GENEALOGY

OF THE

MARSH FAMILY.

OUTLINE FOR

FIVE GENERATIONS.

OF THE FAMILIES OF

JOHN OF SALEM, 1633.
JOHN OF HARTFORD, 1636.
SAMUEL OF NEW HAVEN, 1646.
ALEXANDER OF BRAINTREE, 1654.
JOHN OF BOSTON, 1669, AND
WILLIAM OF PLAINFIELD, 1675.

WITH ACCOUNTS OF THE THIRD FAMILY REUNION AT LAKE PLEASANT IN 1886, EDITED BY D. W. MARSH, OF THE GEN. COM., AND PRINTED, FOR ADDITIONS AND CORRECTIONS, BY THE MARSH FAMILY ASSOCIATION.

AMHERST:
PRESS OF J. E. WILLIAMS.
1886.

JOHN MARSH OF SALEM, 1.

The first Marsh to emigrate from England to America, so far as we have record, took oath in England just before sailing "John Marshe, Mar 24, 1633—34" This was, we suppose, John of Salem. John Marsh appears on record as receiving 20 acres of land at Salem Nov. 2, 1636—37, ch member 1639 wife Susanna ch member 1648. He m Susanna Skelton, dau Rev Samuel, the minister at Salem of the first church in New England after the Pilgrims She d ——. His will, made Mar 20, and probated Nov 26, 1674, indicates that he d Nov, 1674 Est Inv £435 They had

1 Zachary, bap Apr 30 1637
2 John, bap May 9, 1639
3 Ruth, May 5, 1641
4 Benjamin, ——
5 Eliza, Sept 13 1646
6 Ezekiel, Oct 29, 1648

7 Bethiah, Sept 4, 1650
8 Samuel, Oct 2 1652
9 Susanna, May 7, 1654
10 Mary Sept 11, 1656
11 Jacob b Aug 6, 1658, bap Apr 16, 1659

SECOND AND THIRD GENERATIONS.

ZACHARY MARSH 2 (John 1) of Salem, precinct Danvers, freeman 1680, m Aug 15, 1664, Mary Sillsbee, dau Henry of Lynn They had b .

1 John, Nov 26, 1665
2 Mary, Dec. 8, 1666, bap. Oct. 5 1679.
3 Zachary, prob (?) 1668
4 Elizabeth, bap 1670
5 Jonathan, Apr 14, 1672, bap June 4 1672

6 Ebenezer, May 28, 1674
7. Ezekiel bap 1680
8 Abigail, b 1680 or '81, bap Aug 5, 1683
9 Benjamin, bap Nov. 10, 1687

JOHN MARSH 2 (John 1) of Salem (Danvers), m by Maj Hathorne to Sarah Younge Mar 20, 1662, had

(perhaps) 1 The dau John Marsh, bap June 12, 1664 "
2. Sarah,
3 Ruth, Aug, 1668

He d Aug, 1668 in Barbadoes, (Inv Estate £300), and his wid. m (2) 1671, Nicholas Chatwell

BETHIAH MARSH 2 (John 1) of Salem, m Jan 1, 1671, (by Essex Rep m Nov 1, 1673), Jonathan Sillsbee, of Salem. They had b

1. Sarah, Dec 5, 1674
2 Child b and d. Feb. 16, 1677.
3 Jonathan, Mar 16, 1678

4 Bethia, Apr 12, 1680, d æ 1
5 Eliz , Aug. 2, 1685
6. Hannah, Oct 3, 1687

SAMUEL MARSH 2 (John 1) of Salem, m Aug 14, 1679, Priscilla Tompkins, and, to their lasting honor, we have this record In 1691 Samuel Marsh & Priscilla his wife & Zachary Marsh & Mary his wife protest for those condemned'" They had b .

1. Susannah, b May 12, 1680
2. John, b Sept. 1, 1681
3 Hannah, b Sept 18, 1683

4 Sarah, July 18, 1685
5 Margaret, Apr 8, 1688
6 Elizabeth, bap June, 1693

All but Sarah were bap June, 1693

THIRD AND FOURTH GENERATIONS

JOHN MARSH 3 (Zachary 2, John 1) of Danvers, perhaps (?) m the Hannah (?) who was bap " adult " · 1726, Hannah, wife of John " He had property by will of Henry Silsbee, his grandfather He sold prob as " John, Sr " m 1725—6, Mar 16, æ. 60, for £300, 34 acres of land to Ebenezer his brother, æ 51, land bounded by that of Ebenezer, Jonathan, æ 53, and Ezekiel, æ 45, (all Marshes) and probably his brothers As senior he had b

1 John, b (?) abt 1690 (·), prob rem after selling where?
(prob ·) 2 Benjamin, abt 1702 (?), rem to Sutton, Mass

MARY MARSH 3 (Zach 2, John 1) m. Mar. 11, 1689, Ebenezer Cutler She d abt 1729

ZACHARY MARSH 3 (Zachary 2, John 1) of Salem. m. [1(?)]—— and (he or son) m (2) Sept 2 1724, Abigail Moulton, had.

(perhaps) Zachary (·) and perhaps Benjamin of Sutton, who as nephew of Benjamin the first of Sutton, must have been son of either John 3 or Zach 3, sons of Zach 2, John 1 Perhaps he was also father of David, who also must have been his son or son of John 3

ELIZABETH MARSH 3 (Zachary 2, John 1) of Salem, m Dec 5, 1696, Samuel King

JONATHAN MARSH 3 (Zach. 2, John 1) of Danvers, Salem a Narragansett soldier, wounded by Indians Aug. 29, 1708, m (1) May 20, 1697 Mary Very, (2) Hannah Buffington Oct 7, 1725, and had .

1 Jonathan   2 Joseph   3 Samuel   4 Mary
(perhaps had?) Catherine and Hannah, bap Mar 31, 1728

EBENEZER MARSH 3 (Zach 2, John 1) of Danvers, m (1) Nov 25, 1700 Elice Booth, per (?) m (2) Deliverance French, Sept 13, 1725. Who can give descendants?

(prob?) 1. Ebenezer

EZEKIEL MARSH 3 (Zach 2, John 1) of Danvers, m July 1, 1702, Rebecca Gould. They had

1 Desire, bap July 10, 1709   4 Rebecca bap Oct 20, 1717
2 Ezekiel, " May 27, 1711   5. Abigail
3 Daniel, " June 5, 1715   6. Zachariah

ABIGAIL MARSH 3 (Zach 2, John 1) of Danvers, d. unm , her funeral Sept. 22, 1767, æ 87, and so b. 1680 or 1681.

BENJAMIN MARSH 3 (Zach 2, John 1) of Danvers, m Sutton, Mass , 1716, and with William and Jonathan King first three families settled there, 1718, prob m (1) abt 1700-5, Hannah King, b Apr. 15, 1781, and m (2) June 21, 1709, Mary King, dau's of John of Danvers He m (3) Feb 11, 1718. Elizabeth Wheeler. He had

1 Benjamin, m. June 1, 1729   4. Mary, May 30, 1720.
2 Hannah,   m.   1732   5 Lydia, Oct   1722
3 Abigail, b Sept 29, 1718, first child in Sutton

FOURTH AND FIFTH GENERATIONS

BENJAMIN MARSH 4 (either John 3, or Zach 3, Zach 2, John 1) of Danvers and Sutton, Mass , m (1) (?) , m. (2) Aug. 7, 1735, Desire Moulton of Danvers, m (3) Nov 26, 1783, his cousin, Mrs Abigail (Marsh) Harback, dau Benjamin Marsh 3, and had
1 Benjamin, b abt 1720-2   2 Desire, Aug 5, 1737
What others?

JONATHAN MARSH 4 (Jonathan 3, Zachary 2, John 1) m Apr 7, 1726-7, Esther Osborne With some question, the following are their children.

(?) 1 Jonathan, b Salem 1728 or 1729, m Hannah Holt July 20, 1749, rem to Rowe, Mass, and d there Mar 1, 1815, in the 87th year of his age

(²) 2 His sister Esther, who m Benjamin Coats res New Fane, Vt
(²) 3 Zebadiah, who m a sister of Benjamin Coats, and res New Fane, Vt
(²) 4 Samuel b Salem 1735, res Killingly, Ct, Barre and Royalston, Mass, and
      lived long and d in Croydon, N H, in 1832, æ 91
(²) 5 John, b abt 1715, d at New Fane, Vt, æ 93
(²) 6 Martha, m (1) ——— Coates (2) Ezekiel Cutler

JOSEPH MARSH 4 (Jonathan 3, Zach 2, John 1) of Danvers, m
Provided Gould, June 8, 1721 They had:
1 Joseph,   m Elizabeth Parrott, Oct 31, 1753

SAMUEL MARSH 4 (Jona 3, Zach 2, John 1) of Danvers, m Feb
23, 1726, Elizabeth Flint   They had
1 Elizabeth, bap 1730

EBENEZER MARSH 4 (prob Ebenezer 3, Zach 2, John 1) of Killingly, Ct, m Oct 16, 1727, Sarah Stimson of Danvers

EZEKIEL MARSH 4 (Ezekiel 3, Zach 2, John 1) m 1732, Sarah
Buthington, b 1716, d 1809 æ 83 He d Apr, 1798, æ 88 They had:
1 Desire, bap 1736 m Hezekiah   3 Stephen, ———.
  Dunkle   4 Sarah, bap Feb 10, 1750
2 Ezekiel, b Jan 26, 1740   5 John b May 26, 1750

BENJAMIN MARSH 4 (Benj 3, Zach 2, John 1) of Sutton, Mass.,
m (1) Jan 3, 1729, Mehitabel King; m (2) Ruth Waters, had
1 Hannah, Oct 9, 1729   4. Ruth, Mar. 1, 1740
2 Mehitabel, May 8 1731   5. Tamar, Nov 17, 1743
3 Stephen, Dec 20, 1735   6 Elizabeth, Dec 3, 1745

JOHN MARSH OF HARTFORD, 1,

of England 1609 (?)—35, Hartford 1636—60, Hadley 1660—68, who m abt 1612 Anne dau Gov John Webster, came to Hartford, Ct , according to Savage, in 1636, and his name is found in the official record of Hartford's "earliest settlers " He is prob the John Marsh who left Eng. aged 20 in the Plain John, Robt Sayres, Master, May 15, 1635 If so he was b 1609 His parentage is not known He left a brother and three sisters in England as appears by a paper now in Ct. State Archives which gives power of attorney from John's children and niece to a friend in London This paper recalls the terms of the will of John's brother, Joseph Marsh of Braintree, Essex Co , Eng , and suggests the prob. order and approximate times of birth of the brothers and sisters in England.

1 Joseph Marsh, b abt 1605, (?) Will dated 1676
2 Mary, b abt 1607, (?) m John Shores, d between 1676 and 1696
3 John, b abt 1609, (?) sailed for New England 1635, d 1688
4 Lydia b abt 1611, ( ) m ——— Martin, d between 1676 and 1696
5 Grace, b abt 1613, ( ) m Nathaniel Tyres and d March 15, 1696.

Joseph's will mentions "my kinsman Joseph Marsh" Lydia Marsh Martin had a dau Grace Martin, who came to her uncle John Marsh in Hadley, Mass , and m Aug 27, 1676 Nathaniel Phelps of Northampton, Mass , and so gave a tinge of Marsh blood to the Phelps and Huntington families of Hadley including the Bishop With John Marsh's children she received her portion of the Joseph Marsh estate

JOHN MARSH 1, m (1) abt 1612 at Hartford, Ct , Anne, dau Gov John Webster. They had eight children all born at Hartford before they rem to Hadley in 1660.

1. John, b abt 1643, m. 1666, d 1727. 5. Jonathan, b. abt 1650, m 1676, d
2 Samuel, b abt 1645, m 1667, d 1728   1730
3 Joseph, bap Jan 24, 1647, d. y.   6. Daniel, b abt 1653, m 1676, d 1725.
4 Joseph, bap July 15, 1649, d y   7 Grace b prob. 1655, m 1673, d. 1676
              8 Hannah, b prob 1657, m 1675, d 1760

In 1660 Hartford gave the Jews who lived in John Marsh's house liberty to remain seven months Shortly after the family removal to

Hadley, Anne Webster Marsh d June 9, 1662, and John Marsh m
(2) Oct. 7, 1664, Hepzibah Lyman, wid Richard   They had
9   Lydia, b. Oct. 9, 1667, m 1692

John Marsh's will shows by commencing " I John Marsh of Hadley," that he did not return to H[d] and he " d at Windsor 1688 " His
wife Hepzibah d abt. 1684.

SECOND GENERATION.

JOHN MARSH 2, (son John 1), m (1) Nov 28, 1666 Sarah
Lyman, dau Richard Lyman and Hepzibah Ford who became his
father's 2d wife. He d 1727, æ 85   They went to Hartford and
res. on the old Marsh homestead and had .

1 John, b 1668, m. 1695, d. 1741	7. Ebenezer, bap Feb 23, 1679
2. Nathaniel, bap March 5, 1671, d	8 Hannah, bap Apr 10, 1681
1715	9 Ruth, (?) m Wm Cadwell,
3. Joseph, bap. March 5, 1671	Oct 31, 1711
4 Sarah, bap. Feb 17, 1673, m 1694	10. Lydia, bap Jan 13, 1681
John Merrill.	11. Hepzibah, bap June 6, 1686, m
5. Elizabeth, bap. June 27, 1675	1711, Jonathan Wadsworth
6 Hannah, bap Dec 2, 1677, d young	12. Jonathan, bap Aug 7, 1688, d 1783

Sarah Lyman Marsh d. sometime between 1688 and 1707   She
received 10£, by her mother Hepzibah Lyman Marsh's will

John Marsh 2 (John 1) m. (2) Jan. 1, 1708, Susannah Butler
They had
13. Susannah, b Feb. 5, 1710—11.

" Susannah wife John d Dec. 24, 1714 "—Hart records

SAMUEL MARSH 2 (John 1) res. Hatfield, Mass , freeman 1690,
rep 1705 and 1706, d. Sept. 7, 1728, æ 83, m May 6. 1667, Mary
Allison who d Oct. 13, 1720, æ. 78.   They had .

1 Mary, b. Feb 27, 1668	7 Thomas, b. Jan 10, 1680
2 Samuel, b Feb 11, 1670	8 Hannah, b Sept 18, 1681, m Rich
3 John, b. Nov. 6, 1672	Billings
4 Rachel, Oct 15, 1674, m John Wells.	9 Elizabeth, b July 31, 1683, m May-
5 Grace, b Jan 7, 1677, m Thos.	nard Day.
Goodwin	10. Ruth, b. June 16, 1685
6. Mary, b. May 24, 1678, m. Joseph	11 Ebenezer, b May 1, 1687
Morton.	

JONATHAN MARSH 2 (John 1) res Hadley, Mass , freeman 1690
rep. 1701, d. July 3. 1730, æ 80, m 1676, Dorcas, wid Azariah

Dickinson, slain in Swamp fight Aug. 5, 1675. She d. Aug 15, 1723, æ 69 They had

1 Dorcas, b Dec 29, 1677, m July 4, 1700 Ichabod Porter

2 Ann, b Sept 15, 1680, m June 21, 1698 Samuel Cook.

3 Mary, b Feb 9, 1683 m abt 1703 William Dickinson

4 Jonathan, b Aug 7, 1685, Min. Windsor, Ct

5 Sarah b. Dec 4, 1687, m Nov 1716 Noah Cook

6 Hannah, b Feb 12, 1690, m Oct 17, 1711, Samuel Dickinson

7 Daughter, b July 27, 1692, d æ 2 days

8 Son, b Sept 14, 1693, d Sept, 1698

DANIEL MARSH 2 (John 1) res Hadley, at the original homestead, freeman 1690, rep 1692, and often after d. Feb. 24, 1725, æ. 72, m Nov 5, 1676, Hannah dau Wm Lewis, and wid Samuel Crow, slain in Falls fight, May 18, 1676 They had

1 Daniel Oct 29, 1677, d unm Feb 15 1770, æ 92

2 John, Mar 9, 1679

3 Joseph, Jan 16, 1685.

4 Ebenezer, Apr 22, 1688

5 Job, June 11, 1690

6. Hannah, May 17, 1694, m Oct 17, 1711, Daniel Kent

7 William, Jan. 3, 1697.

GRACE MARSH 2 (John 1) of Hadley, m. Jan. 26, 1673 Timothy Baker, son of Edward of Lynn and Northampton She d May 31, 1676 They res Northampton and had :

1. Grace, b 1673 and d Feb 10, 1673. 2. Timothy, b. 1675, d. y.

HANNAH MARSH 2 (John 1) of Hadley. m Jan 28, 1675 Joseph Loomis 3 of Windsor, Ct (John 2, Joseph 1). They had

1 Hannah, b Jan 10, 1678

2 Ann, "   "   "

3 Joseph, Feb 13, 1681

4 Joseph, Nov 28 1682

5 Grace, Mar 17, 1685.

6 Lydia Apr 15, 1686, d æ 16

7 Sarah, Jan 8, 1693

Hannah Marsh Loomis d. Aug 22, 1760.

LYDIA MARSH 2 (John 1) of Hadley, m Dec 8, 1692, David Loomis of Windsor, Ct As youngest child she rec £20, a double portion in her mother's will They had

1 Lydia, Oct 21, 1693

2 David, Dec. 2, 1694

3 Aaron, Sept 5, 1696

4 Hepzibah Dec 2, 1698

5 Chakim, July 27, 1701

6 Elizabeth, Sept 26, 1704

7 Richard, Jan 1, 1707

8 Hannah, Aug 2, 1709

THIRD GENERATION

JOHN MARSH 3 (John 2, John 1) res Hartford and pioneer Litchfield, Ct , m (1) Dec 12, 1695 Mabel Pratt, who d June 6, 1696
He m (2) Jan 6, 1698 Elizabeth Pitkin   They had .

1 John, Jan 31, 1699, d 1812, æ 13   6 Isaac, Nov 8 1710
2 Ebenezer, Nov 3, 1701   7 John, Oct 20, 1712
3. Elizabeth Nov 20, 1703, m Jno Bird   8 Timothy, Oct 1, 1714
4. William, June, 1706   9 Hezekiah, Apr 26, 1720
5 George. Feb 1708

John Marsh 3 d. Oct 1, 1744. Elizabeth Pitkin Marsh d Hartford, Dec 1, 1718, and then gravestones still stand by Centre
church

LIEUT. NATHANIEL MARSH 3 (John 2. John 1) res Hartford, m
Elizabeth Spencer abt. 1701( )   They had

1. Nathaniel, bap Dec 2, 1705   4 Hannah, bap. Jan 18, 1712
2 Samuel bap July 20, 1707   5 Lemuel, bap, May 9, 1718
3 David, bap Oct 30, 1709

Lieut. Nathaniel Marsh d ——, 1748

CAPT. JOSEPH MARSH 3 (John 2, John 1) twin Nathaniel, a pro-
prietor at Lebanon Ct , 1697, m abt. 1696( ) at Hartford, (where
his 1st and 2d children were baptized in 2d ch) to Hannah ——
They had

1 Elizabeth, bap Jan 30 1697—8   4 Pelatiah, Dec 8, 1707
2 Joseph, bap Dec 10, 1699,   5 Jonathan Sept. 23, 1713
3 Hannah, Nov 9, 1701
  Chil 3, 4 and 5 b. at Lebanon, Ct

JONATHAN MARSH 3 (John 2, John 1) Capt , Explorer New Hartford, Ct , 1733. and rem there, one of first settlers abt 1736, and
d. there May 1783   M. (1) Sarah Wadsworth of Hartford, dau
Jonathan, who left m his will £10 each to her 3 children   They
were ·

1 Jonathan, b 1715   2 Joseph, bap 1718(?)   3 Elizabeth, b abt 1720(?)

   He m (2) Elizabeth Loomis of Windsor, prob m 1736   They
had

4 .John, b 1727   6 .Job 17_9   8 Eunice, 1736   10 Hannah, 1747
5. Sarah, b 1728   7 Moses 1731   9 Lois, 1743

SAMUEL MARSH 3 (Samuel 2, John 1) of Hatfield, b. Feb 11, 1670   No information

JOHN MARSH 3 (Samuel 2 John 1) b Hatfield, Nov 6, 1672 Perhaps (?) the John who was of Sunderland 1721, and conveyed his homestead to the town in 1741, and d Jan 11 1744   Was Mary Marsh his widow?

THOMAS MARSH 3 (Samuel 2, John 1) res Hatfield and Ware Mass d 1759, m 1702, Mary Trumbull of Suffield, Ct   His children all b at Hatfield, and the family rem to Ware abt 1730

1 Thomas May 1, 1703, d unm 1728
2 Mary, Oct 27, 1704
3. Samuel,   1706
4 Rachel,   1708
5 Ruth, Feb 15, 1710
6 Judith July 25 1712
7 Joseph, Apr 14, 1714
8 Ephraim, Jan 5, 1717
9 Daniel, June 12, 1719, insane
10 Martha, Apr 12, 1721

His wid prob the Mary Marsh of Cong ch records, who d June 25, 1765

EBENEZER MARSH 3 (Sam 2, John 1) rem to Sunderland and d Sept. 9, 1717   He m Elizabeth Gillett   They had

1 Ebenezer, d y
2 Elizabeth, June 4, 1710
3. Ephraim, June 12, 1712, d Aug 1, 1714
4 Esther July 15, 1714
5 Ebenezer,   1716
6 Ephraim,   1718
7 Enos,   1720
8 Dorothy,   1723
9 Mary,   1725
10 Thankful,   1728
11 Hannah   1733

REV JONATHAN MARSH (Jonathan 2, John 1) grad Harvard 1705, settled at Windsor, Ct , June 1710, at first colleague of Rev Mr Mather, and rem till death, Sept 8, 1717, æ. 62   He m July 13, 1710, Margaret Whiting, b Jan 5, 1690, d Aug 8, 1717   She was dau. Joseph Whiting, who m (1) Mary Pynchon; (2) m 1776, Anna Allyn, both granddaughters of William Pynchon of Springfield, Mass   They had

1 Margaret, b June 10 1711, m Rev Nath'l Roberts of Torrington, d Oct 1, 1717, æ 36
2 Jonathan, Jan 1, 1714
3 Mary, July 19, 1716, m Rev Stephen Heaton of Goshen, Ct
4 Dorcas, Aug 31, 171-, m Jabez Bissell, Windsor, Ct.
5 Hannah May 28, 1723
6 Joseph Nov 10, 1727
7 Ann, Jan 28 1730

2

DANIEL MARSH 3 (Daniel 2, John 1) d. unm. Feb. 15, 1770, æ 92

JOHN MARSH 3 (Daniel 2, John 1) of Hadley, m (1) June 27,
1704, Joanna Porter, (2) Feb 2, 1715, Hannah Barnard, b June
8, 1684, d Sept 31, 1716, æ 32, m (3) Oct 9, 1718, Sarah Williams,
dau Isaac Jones and Judith Cooper, b Oct 2, 1688 He d Sept 2,
1725, and his wid prob m (2) July 28, 1732, James Grey, and d
June 1, 1759 Children

1 John b Aug 25, 1710, d y
2 Abigail
3 Martha.
4 Anne
5 John, d July 3, 1726, æ 3
6 Judith, d Nov 1, 1725, æ 8 mos

REV JOSEPH MARSH 3 (Daniel 2, John 1) of Hadley and Bram-
tree (now Quincy, Mass); grad Har Coll 1705, pastor 1st ch
Braintree from May 18, 1709 till d Mar 8, 1725-6, in 41st yr of
his age, m June 30, 1709, Ann Fiske, dau Rev Moses Fiske
They had

1 Joseph, b Dec, 1710, H C 1728,
   taught many eminent men at Quincy,
   Mass
2 Daniel, July 27, 1712
3 Hannah, July 10, 1716, bap Feb 13
4 Mary, bap Feb 2, 1718, m. May 19,
   1746, Rev Jedediah Adams
5 Anne, Apr. 19, 1772, d y
6 Anne, Oct 23, 1723, m July 11,
   1762, Col Josiah Quincy

EBENEZER MARSH 3 (Daniel 2, John 1) of Hadley, d 1772, m.
(1) 1710, Mary Parsons, who d July 2, 1759, m (2) Miriam ——,
who d July 30, 1765, in her 63d year They had.

1 Elisha, May 27, 1713
2 Mary,   1715, d 1796, m Dr
   Ezekiel Porter of Wethersfield, Ct
3 Ebenezer,   m 1716, d 1795
4 Hannah, m Samuel Ely of Lyme, Ct,
      (had three children)
5 Jonathan,   m 1747, d 1766
6 John,   m 1749

CAPT JOB MARSH 3 (Daniel 2, John 1), town clerk, Hadley,
1727-47, m. (1) Sept 24, 1713, Mehitabel Porter, dau Hon Samuel
of Hadley She was b. Sept 12, 1694, and d July 13, 1739, æ 44
He m. (2) Sept 19, 1742, Rebecca Pratt, at Hartford, Ct He d
Aug 29, 1746 He had

1 Dau b and d Oct. 18, 1714
2 Moses, Mar 20, 1718
3 Samuel, Apr 19, 1721
4 Daniel, Jan 28, 1725
5 Putz, Oct 25, 1729.
6 Joseph, Nov 6, 1743

WILLIAM MARSH 3 (Daniel 2, John 1) of Hadley, d Nov. 3,
1727, m Feb 28, 1722, Hannah, dau Experience Porter Children:

1 William, d 1726   2 William, b 1727 d. unm Mansfield, Ct

FOURTH GENERATION

COL. EBENEZER MARSH 4 (John 3, John 2, John 1) of Litchfield, Ct., Judge of Probate, Judge Co. Court, Rep forty-eight sessions, m. abt 1725, Deborah Buell He d. Apr., 1773, æ 71 ys. and 5 mos. She d July, 1784, æ 77 They had born

1 Deborah, Nov 9, 1726, m Nicholas McCall
2. Elizabeth Feb 10, 1729-30, m Nathaniel Goodwin
3 Lois, Mar 3 1731 m Mark Prindle, who d May 25, 1804, æ 70
4 Hannah, Mar 24, 1733, m (1) Edward Phelps, (2) Mark Prindle
5 Solomon, Feb 10, 1735-6
6 Ebenezer, Mar 4 1737, d May 12, 1737
7 Anna, May 25, 1738, m her cousin John Marsh 4 (John 3)
8 Ebenezer, Oct 7, 1740, m (1) his cousin, Rhoda Marsh, (2) Lucy Phelps
9 Ozias, Apr 5, 1713, d 1760
10 Hepzibah, Aug 29, 1745, m Dr Samuel Catlin
11 John, Jan 4, 1748, d Jan 3, 1751
12 Molly, Nov 24, 1752, m Moses Seymour

CAPT WILLIAM MARSH 4 of Litchfield (John 3, John 2, John 1), m Nov 9, 1733, Susannah Webster They had b

1. Ann, June 23, 1735, m Abner Baldwin
2 Susannah, Jan 16, 1736-7.
3 Irene, Oct 4, 1738, m David Welch.
4 William, Sept. 14, 1740, m Esther Roe (No issue)

GEORGE MARSH 4 John 3, John 2, John 1) of Litchfield, Ct, m June 16, 1731, Lydia Bird They had b :

1 Ambrose, Feb 27, 1732		5 Elijah	
2 Roger, Oct, 31, 1733		6 Ambrose	
3 Adam, Aug 4, 1735		7 Titus	
4. George, Sept 25, 1736, m Catherine Kilborn		8 Lydia,	m Joshua Garrett, Jr
		9 Sabra,	m Abel Camp

CAPT JOHN MARSH 4, (John 3, John 2, John 1) of Litchfield and Morris, Ct, rep in leg. d Morris, Ct, Dec. 27, 1780, æ 69 He m Sarah ———— They had b.

1 John, Oct 17, 1733, d Dec 3, 1806, æ 73
2 Jerusha, Oct 23, 1735, m Solomon Marsh her cousin
3 Elizabeth, m. July 11, 1761, Col Bezaleel Beebe of Litchfield
4 Rachel, m Rev Geo Beckwith
5 Rhoda, m Ebenezer Marsh, Jr, her cousin
6 Mary, m Benjamin Stone, Jr
7 Sarah, ( ) m Dr Seth Bird

QUARTERMASTER GEN. ISAAC MARSH 4, and com in chief of the troops in Ct., (John 3, John 2, John 1) of Litchfield, m Dec 23, 1735, Susannah Pratt He d. March 8, 1788, æ 79, she d. Apr 6, 1788, æ. 76 They had b

1 Elizabeth,   m Roswell McNiel
2 Isaac, Sept 11, 1736, m Martha Lyman
3 Ruth, May 14, 1738, m John Wadhams
4. Elisha, Nov 15, 1742, m Honor Beckley
5 Sally   m David King
6 Susannah, Aug 20, 1746, m Gen T Skinner.

TIMOTHY MARSH 4 (John 3, John 2, John 1) of Litchfield, Ct., m —— Nott They had b

1 Timothy,   m Sarah ——

HEZEKIAH MARSH 4 (John 3, John 2, John 1) of Hartford. Ct., d. 1791, æ 71, m (1) Dec 1, 1711, Christian Edwards, b 1727, d June 16, 1770, d m John, m (2) Elizabeth Jones wid. Levi, of Hartford, m (3) Hannah Tiley, wid Saml, she d 1789. Children

1 Jerusha, b Aug 28 171- (-) m Sept 22, 1768 Joseph Wadsworth
2. John, b Nov 6, 1719, d Dec 8, 1719
3. Abigail, b Nov. 29, 1750, m Theodore Skinner
4 John, b Oct 4, 1753, m Susan Bunce
5 Christian, b Aug 8, 1755, m Capt Chas Merrill
6 An unnamed son, b and d 1759
7. Anne, b June 10, 1761, m (1) —— Bunce, (2) John Packwood
8 Hezekiah, b March 2, 1763, m 1790, Sarah Burnham.

NATHANIEL MARSH 4 (Nath 3, John 2, John 1,) of Hartford, m (?) Child b

Samuel, bap May 9, 1731

ENSIGN DANIEL MARSH 4 (Nath 3, John 2, John 1) of East Hartford, m Irene Bigelow, b 1711, d March 27, 1790, in 79th year He d. 1793 in 85th year They had b
1 Daniel,   1731   2 "Cate," who d Oct, 1759

LEMUEL MARSH 4 (Nath 3, John 2, John 1) of Hartford, m Bathsheba —— They had

1. Mary,   d Jan 8, 1751, after her father's death
ENSIGN JOSEPH MARSH 4, of Lebanon, Ct (Joseph 3, John 2, John 1) b Hartford, Dec 5, 1699, bap Hartford 1st ch Dec 10,
2

1699, m Mercy Bill Sept 25, 1723   He d 1753 m Lebanon, Ct ,
where he lived, she d 1811 m Hartford, Vt   They had b

    1 Mercy, 1725, m Israel Loomis,   1717
    2 Joseph, Jan 12, 1726   7 m Jan 10, 1750 - 51, Dorothy Mason
    3 Anna,   1729, m   1752 Pelatiah Marsh, Jr
    4 Abel,   1735, m   1756, Dorothy Udall, Stonington
    5 Elisha   1738, m   —— Terry
    6 Eliphalet

These four sons and widowed mother, rem to Hartford, Vt m
1773 or 4

PELATIAH MARSH 4 of Lebanon (Joseph 3, John 2, John 1) m
May 10, 1731 Mary Moore of Southold   They had b .

1. Pelatiah, April 11, 1732   5 Silus, March 3, 1710
2 Mary, Dec 22, 1733   6 Jesse, Sept 3, 1713
3 Lucy, Feb 11, 1736   7 ( ), March 31, 1716
4. Isaiah, Feb 3, 1738 ·

He rem from Lebanon to Sharon, Ct m 1764, and d there 1790,
æ 83

JONATHAN MARSH 4 of Lebanon, Ct (Joseph 3, John 2, John 1),
m (1) m 1733, Alice Newcomb, m. (2) Dec 1, 1752, Keziah
Phelps   Children b :

1 Elizabeth, July 26, 1735   5 Joel, June 1, 1745
2 Hannah, Nov 20, 1736   { 6 Zebulon, May 12, 1748
3 John, Mar 10, 1739   { 7 Sarah May 12, 1745
4. Abraham, May 31, 1742   8 Alice, Oct 11, 1753

JONATHAN MARSH 4 of New Hartford, Ct (Jonathan 3, John 2,
John 1) b. Hartford, 1715, rem when 21 with his father to New
Hartford, farmer; m Apr 4, 1745, Theodocia Kellogg, dau Isaac,
d Jan 12, 1802, æ 87, wife d Mar 6, 1795   They had b

    1 Theodocia, July 13, 1717, m (1) Aug 9, 1767, John Gilbert, rem to Her-
       kimer, N Y , m (2) 1795, Capt Cook, res Sullivan and d at Cazeno-
       via, N Y
    2 Ruth, July 14, 1749 d unm Mar 7, 1813
    3 Chloe, Nov 12 1750, m Elijah Flower, Jr , Capt Rev War , rem to New
       Hartford, N Y , abt 1791, no children
    4 Mary, July 22, 1751 m Elijah Seymour, s of John, July 3, 1777, rem
       1791 or 1792 to New Hartford N Y thence to Marcellus and Skeneat-
       teles, where he d 1806, and she 1839, æ 81 ys 10 mos , 27 days, 8
       children

5. Jonathan, Mar 1, 1757, m Damaris Pitkin, b New Hartford, Oct 12,
1756, dau Caleb. He was farmer, carpenter, often representative and
selectman, member of convention in 1718 which formed present constitu-
tion of Ct., d New Hartford Jan 27, 1888, æ 80 She d Aug 12, 1830
They were parents of Rev Frederick Marsh, who lived 92 ys, and seven
others.
6. Elizabeth, Oct 13, 1759, m May 6, 1778, Roger Sheldon, b. Windsor, Ct.,
March, 1756, res New Hartford and Pine Meadow, rem 1809 to Huron,
N. Y She d Sept 25, 1845, eleven children
7 Ashbel, July 11, 1762, m Somers, Ct. Nov 27, 1783, Abigail Ward, b
1767, res New Hartford and d where b Nov. 19, 1815. She d New
Hartford, Aug. 10, 1816, eight children
8. Cynthia, Apr. 13, 1765, m. New Hartford, Feb 13, 1791, Rufus Northway,
res. New Hartford, N Y , and from abt 1835, both, with dau. Mrs Whi-
ton at Ithaca, N Y., where she d Mar. 3, and he Feb 10, 1840 six
children

JOSEPH MARSH 4 of New Hartford (Jonathan 3, John 2, John 1)
d. unm. Dec. 21, 1812, æ. nearly 94

JOHN MARSH 4 of New Hartford (Jonathan 3, John 2, John 1)
m. (1) Feb. 2, 1758, Lucina Seymour, who d. May 14, 1762, m
(2) June 17, 1763, Sarah Nash, b. New Hartford, Apr. 26, 1738,
d. July 17, 1775, m. (3) Nov 27, 1777, Mrs Miriam Sedgwick
(wid. Wm), b. abt 1729 Before 1800, with son James he rem.
to Bridgwater, N. Y , and d there Nov 10, 1805, æ 78 She d.
West Hartford, Ct , Sept 17, 1819, æ 90

SARAH MARSH 4 (Jonathan 3, John 2, John 1) m. Abraham Kellogg, b. 1720 (s. Isaac), res New Hartford. She d. abt 1796, æ
abt. 68. He d. Jan 13, 1805. They had nine children.

JOB MARSH 4 of New Hartford, Ct. (Jonathan 3, John 2, John 1)
m. Jemima ———, b 1728, d. Jan 15, 1810, æ 82 He d. Sept
12, 1822, æ. 93 They had b :

1. Job, May 12, 1755, m 1781, Salome Beach, b June 16, 1763, d. Jan 7,
1842 He was soldier in Rev , d Apr 20, 1835, æ 80. They had eight
children
2 Amos. 3. Lucretia 4 Roswell, b 1760, m Anna Crow, d Sept 26 1843
5 Elijah, in navy during Rev War, captured and paroled at St Christophers,
Carribee Is., Dec 29, 1779 He ret home and d unm

MOSES MARSH 4 of New Hartford (Jonathan 3, John 2, John 1)
m. 1757, Sarah Merrill He d abt 1790, æ. 60. They had b .

1. Sarah,   m David Covil; rem. West.
2 Anna, m. Allen Goodwin, and had Horace, silversmith, Hartford
3 Amy, m Eli Seymour, West Hartford, Ct.
4 Lucy, twin to Amy, m Theodore Lee
5 Lois, m John Seymour, rem to Black River, N. Y. State
6 Hannah   7 Moses of Hartford, d Sept 27, 1794, æ 24 or 25
Three others d y

Lois Marsh 4 of New Hartford (Jonathan 3, John 2, John 1)
m. (1) Rev Ebenezer Davenport of Greenwich, Ct., m. (2) Judge
Hugh White (first settler Whitesborough, N. Y.)   She rem. there
abt 1754, d. Apr. 13, 1829, æ. 86.   They had b. five sons and three
daughters.

Dan C., Joseph, Hugh, Ansel Philo, Rachel, Aurelia, and Polly.

Hannah Marsh 4 of New Hartford, Ct (Jonathan 3, John 2,
John 1) m Thomas Wadsworth of Hartford, Ct , after he d she
rem to her sister, Mrs White of Whitesborough, N. Y, till her
death, then lived with her nephew, Dea James Marsh of Bridgwater,
N. Y., d. Feb. 19, 1840, æ. 93   Only one child, dau., who d æ. 17.

Samuel Marsh 4 of Ware, Mass (Thomas 3, Samuel 2, John 1)
m Jan 18, 1731-2, Zeruiah Thomas, dau. William, d. abt. 1745,
when his wid m (2) Mar 2, 1746-7, Isaiah Piatt, son John   She
d. Apr 18, 1798.   Children b. :

1 Eunice, Jan. 15, 1733, d y
2. Amos, Nov 15, 1733, m Beulah Leonard of Rutland
3. Mary, June 13, 1735, m Jan 21, 1751, Solomon Emmons of Quobbin
4 Eunice, Nov. 20, 1737.
5 Patience, July 20, 1740, m Apr 5, 1754, Henry Gilbert of Brookfield.
6. { Thankful, Feb 1, 1741-2   8. Miriam, Jan 18, 1743.
7. { Submit, Feb 1, 1741-2   9 Samuel, Feb 18, 1744-5.

Judah Marsh 4 of Ware, Mass. (Thomas 3, Samuel 2, John 1)
d. May 7, 1801, m. Nov 4, 1736, Hannah Olmstead, dau. Jabez, b.
Apr. 22, 1718, d Oct. 20, 1793, had b

1. Elijah, Nov 10, 1737, m Mar. 4, 1759, Elizabeth Daman, d Nov 1, 1765.
2 Joel, Mar 31, 1738
3 Thomas, Aug. 14, 1741, m June 26, 1766, Mary Thomas, d. June 14, 1813
4 Rachel, July 20, 1743, m. Mar 7. 1763, Silas Adams of Brookfield, d. Mar.
   18, 1832
5 Hannah, Mar 13, 1746, m. (1) May 28, 1766, Joseph Luce, m (2) July
   4, 1769, Moses Brown, and d Jan 28 (?) 1816

6 Thankful, Aug. 9, 1748, m William Breckenridge of Ware, and d Dec
  27, 1831.

7 Dorothy, May 29, 1752 m Dec 22, 1768, Thomas Winslow, Jr. of Hardwick, res Ware, d Feb 15, 1829

8 Jonathan, May 7, 1752, m Annah, dau Jacob Pepper, res Ware, d Sept
  16, 1838

9. Mary, bap July 7, 1754

10 Judah May 22, 1757, m (1) Elizabeth Smith, (2) Feb 20, 1800, Jerusha
   Collins, d Feb 10, 1816

11 Joel, July 7, 1759, m Sept 20, 1785, Annis Smith, res Ware and Hardwick, d. April 12, 1804

JOSEPH MARSH 4 of Ware, Mass (Thos 3, Sam 2, John 1) m
May 17, 1750 Abigail Simons, dau Joseph   Had b

1. Samuel, Jan 22, (?) d. Feb. 20, 1790

2 Joseph, July 10, 1753, m Mary Wheeler, dau George, d New Salem, April
  7, 1829

3 Ebenezer, Dec 24, 1755, m dau Mather Gray of Warren.

4. Sarah, June 8, 1758, m a Pratt of Belchertown and murdered by him

5 John, Sept 21, 1760, went to Butternuts, N Y

6 Benjamin, Dec 27, 1764, rem. to Genesee River, N. Y

EPHRAIM MARSH 4, of Ware (Thos. 3, Sam. 2, John 1) children
bap. at Hardwick, m. Oct. 8, 1741, Sarah Olmstead, dau Jabez
They had :

1. Noah, bap April 17, 1743.	3 Sarah, bap. April 28, 1751.
2. Huldah, bap Sept 14, 1746	4 Mary, bap Oct 5, 1755

EBENEZER MARSH 4, of Montague, Mass (Ebenezer 3, Sam. 2,
John 1) prob m Nov. 17, 1741, his cousin Martha Marsh 4 (Thos
3, Sam 2,) b. April 12, 1721. They had b .

1 Joseph,	1742, lived in Conway	5 Ebenezer,	1750, res Montague
2 Israel,	1744, res near Schoharie	6 Martha,	1752.
Bridge		7 Eunice, Aug. 3, 1757	
3 Lydia,	1746.	8 Editha, Oct. 2, 1762	
4. Mary,	1748		

EPHRAIM MARSH 4, of Montague (Ebenezer 3, Sam. 2, John 1)
m. Mar. 24, 1746, Sarah Mattoon of Northfield, b. Feb. 21, 1723
He d. June 27, 1805, æ 89, she d. April 9, 1797. They had b

1. Elizabeth, May 25, 1747	8 Philip, Dec (?) 1759, d June 4, 1761
2 Ebezer, March 28, 1749.	9 Philip, June 2, 1761, d Jan 18, 1772
3 Sarah, Dec. 7, 1750.	10 Samuel, Jan 19, 1763, d Nov 4,
4 Ephraim, Nov 13 1752	1836

5 Rebekah, March 30, 1755, d Feb 1, 11. Esther, Aug 21, 1765, d. May 18,
   1835   1766.
6 Mercy,
7 Thankful, } May 22, 1757

ENOS MARSH 4, of Montague (Ebenezer 3, Samuel 2, John 1) m.
(1) 1751 Judith Hawkes, she d. June 9, 1776, (2) Wid Mary
(Hawkes) Smeed, sis. Judith, she d March 27, 1803, he d. in Montague, Feb 16, 1810, æ 90   Children b.

   1 Enos,   } May 9, 1755, d y
   2 Judith,
   3 Jonathan, Aug 17, 1756, d May 4, 1825, m Freedom Taylor
   4 Judith, Aug 11, 1759, unm
   6 Enos, Mar 18, 1760, m his cousin Mercy Marsh 5, (Ephraim 4)
   7 Joshua, Aug 8, 1763, d Feb 1, 1855, æ. 89 yrs, 5 mos and 23 days   He
     m (1) Dec 30, 1793, Mindwell Crosby, b Oct 25, 1769, d Aug 5, 1808,
     æ. 38 yrs and 10 mos, m (2) Jan. 25, 1809, Abigail Clary, b Sept 20,
     1769, d May 9, 1848, æ· 78 yrs., 7 mos and 19 days

REV JONATHAN MARSH 4 (Rev Jona 3, Jonathan 2, John 1)
of New Hartford, Ct , between 54 and 55 years in min , Y C 1735,
ord or set Oct , 1739, d 1794, æ. 80, m. (1) Elizabeth Sheldon of
Hartford, Feb. 26, 1740, she d. May 20, 1749, m (2) May 22, 1751,
Wid Marianna Keith, with two dau's , sister of John Lawrence,
treas of the colony   Children by each wife six.

   1 Ann,   m. Sept 25, 1759, Capt. Zebulon Seymour of Hartford, d. Nov.,
     1812
   2 Jerusha,   m Joseph King, Middletown
   3 Elizabeth,   m. Jerijah Merrill of New Hartford.
   4 Margaret,   m Luke Cooley
   5 Fanny,   m John Collins
   6 Mary,   m Abner Beech
   7 Hannah,   m (1) Caleb Watson, New Hartford, (2) Wm Ellery,
     Hartford
   8 Joseph Whiting, b 1748, grad Y C., d in West Indies 1764, æ 21
   9. Daniel
   10. Isaac,   m Lucy Smith, dau Dea. Martin, res Tyringham, d 1792.
   11 Jonathan,   d y
   12 John Lawrence,   in 1796, m. Lucy wid. of Isaac.

REV ELISHA MARSH 4, of Westminster, Mass (Ebenezer 3,
Daniel 2, John 1) Grad. H C 1738, Set at Westminster on incor-
poration of the town in 1712, m Wid Deborah (Lorin) Lathrop of
Boston   After 15 years rem to Walpole, Cheshire co., N H and

3

became Judge of court of com. Pleas   Of his descendants I have only his son, Capt. Elisha, grandson Luther, of Pompey, Onondaga co., N Y and his great grandson, Luther Rawson Marsh, Esq. of 48 Wall street, N Y

EBENEZER MARSH 4, of Hadley (Ebenezer 3, Daniel 2, John 1) lived on the old Hadley homestead and d. May 29, 1795, m. Dec 4, 1716, Sarah Eastman who d Jan 31, 1794.   They had b :

1. Timothy, July 6, 1717, d May 12, 1751.
2 Daniel, June 26, 1749, d April 30, 1751
3 Timothy, Oct.5, 1751, m Sept 23, 1779 Mercy Smith, b Oct 26, 1756, dau Windsor, d. Oct 19, 1796
4 Sarah, July 20, 1754, m Dec 9, 1779, Nath Dickinson, Jr Esq of Amherst, and d Dec 9 1801
5. Ebenezer, Sept 8, 1757, d Jan 25, 1761.
6 Elijah, Dec 23, 1760 d Jan 11, 1761.
7 Ebenezer, Jan 5, 1762, d unm abt 1818
8 Mary b and d. May 9, 1765
9. Susanna, b Jan. 26, 1766, d Feb 26, 1766

DR JONATHAN MARSH 4, of Norwich, Ct (Ebenezer 3, Daniel 2, John 1) prob studied at Wethersfield with Dr. Ezekiel Porter, the husband of his sister who practiced medicine for years after her husband's death. Dr. Marsh was in the Northern army 1755—57, in French wars, a skillful surgeon.   He m. Nov. 5, 1747 Sarah Hart of Farmington, Ct , he d June 3, 1766.   They had b. :

1 Sarah, July 27, 1749, m Dr Samuel 4. Hannah, Nov 19, 1757.
  Lee, March 23, 1769.   5 Mary, Nov 11, 1759
2 Abigail, April 8, 1751.   6 Joseph, March 6, 1762.
3 Jonathan, June 15, 1754.

JOHN MARSH 4, of Rocky Hill, Wethersfield, Ct (Ebenezer 3, Daniel 2, John 1) m. recorded at Hadley, Mass., Jan. 17, 1749, Abigail Bulkley.   They had b .

1 Mary, Sept 2, 1749
2. Martha, Nov. 10, 1751, m. Stephen Bulkley, d. April 6, 1804, æ. 53.
3. John, Sept 27, 1753, m Miss Goodrich
4 Rebecca, Nov 2, 1755.   (Did she m. a Wright?)
5 Anna,   m. Simeon Butler of Rocky Hill
6. Eli,   m. and rem. to Unadilla, N Y.

MOSES MARSH 4, of Hadley (Capt. Job 3, Daniel 2, John 1) res. Worthington. Mass , d Oct. 4, 1796, æ. 78, m. Nov. 2, 1739. Hannah Cook.   They had b.

1. Moses, Oct. 22, 1740, d. Aug. 16, 1746.
2. Hannah, Oct 2, 1744, d Aug. 12, 1746.
3. Moses, June 11, 1747, d Nov. 16, 1757
4. Hannah, Feb. 2, 1749, d Sept 15, 1753
5. Job, May 4, 1752, d Jan 26, 1754
6. Mehitable, m. 1780 Sam Cook, prob. d in Morristown, Vt
7. Hannah, m Daniel Marsh and d in Belchertown
8 Joseph, Oct. 26, 1754
9. Job, abt. 1756

SAMUEL MARSH 4, of Hadley (Capt. Job 3, Daniel 2, John 1) d.
Oct. 2, 1760, m. Dec 5, 1745, Phebe Porter, dan. Samuel, b Jan
19, 1720, d Oct 1, 1779, æ 60   They had b .

1. Daughter, b. aud d. Aug 23, 1746.
2 Phebe, m Benom Dickinson of Northfield
3. Rebecca, m. Eleazer Cook, 1cm. to St Albans, Vt.
4 Samuel.

DANIEL MARSH 4, of Hadley (Capt Job 3, Daniel 2, John 1) d.
Jan 4, 1810, æ 84, m 1751, Hannah Parsons, dan Timothy of
Durham, Ct , she d. Feb. 9, 1800, æ 74   They had b. :

1 Mehitabel, Dec 3, 1751, d Aug 30, 1752
2. William, Oct 26, 1753, Sol at cap of Cornwallis, d in Warren unm
3 Sarah, m Joseph Field of Warren
4. Eliphalet, Feb 2, 1761, res. Coleraine and Belchertown
5. Parsons, Sept 7, 1766, "   "   "   "

DR. PEREZ MARSH 4 (Capt. Job 3, Daniel 2, John 1) grad H.
C. 1748, surgeon Lake George 1755, Judge court of Com Pleas,
Berkshire Co , Mass., 16 years 1765—81 res Dalton, Mass , d.
there May 20, 1784, m. abt. 1759, Sarah, dan Col Israel Williams
of Hatfield, Mass , she was b 1736 and d June 2, 1817   They had
b. :

1. Chester, Oct. 1, 1760, m   Abigail Burnham of Wethersfield
2. Sarah, March 28, 1762. m   Israel Peck of Pittsfield, Mass
3. Lucretia, March 20, 1764, d y.
4 Martha, Nov 5, 1765, m.   Thomas Gold of Pittsfield, Mass
5 Eunice, Sept 9, 1767, m   Darius Larned of Pittsfield, Mass
6 Henry, July 18, 1769, d. y
7 Henry, Sept 11, 1771, m April, 1796, Betsey Lawrence, d in Rev Micah
8. Lucretia, Jan 9, 1774, m Nov 8, 1791 Capt Wm Henry Mellen of Pitts-
    field, Mass , son of Col James
9 Elizabeth, Sept 8, 1776, m Capt Jonathan Allen, son of Rev Thos of
    Pittsfield, Mass
10. Harriet, July 31, 1779.
11. Christopher, Aug. 31, 1782

JONATHAN AND SAMUEL MARSH OF NEW HAVEN, CT. AND THEIR DESCENDANTS.

FIRST AND SECOND GENERATION

JONATHAN MARSH 1, appears upon New Haven records as early as 1643 He took oath 1644, was a miller, appears at Milford, Ct 1649, also 1654—57 and at Norwalk, Ct. 1657—1664. He had b. both at Milford :

1 John, Feb 7, 1653—54   2 Jonathan, Sept. 29, 1657

FIRST AND SECOND GENERATION.

SAMUEL MARSH 1, appears upon New Haven records in 1616, took oath 1647, had there sister ' Goodwife Fuller," and had b there .

1. Mary,   1648   5 Elizabeth, Dec 27, 1657
2. Samuel, Feb. 12, 1650   6 John, May 2, 1661
3 Comfort, Aug 22, 1652   7 Joseph, April 1, 1663
4 Hannah, July 22, 1655

He removed with wife and seven children to Elizabethtown, N. J with first settlers, abt 1665 or 6, and d. 1683

SECOND AND THIRD GENERATION.

SAMUEL MARSH 2 (Samuel 1) rem to Philadelphia

JOHN MARSH 2 (Samuel 1) of Eastside Rahway River, N J near the Sound, m " Mary Connally from Ireland " They had a large family of whom was .

1 Daniel.

JOSEPH MARSH 2 (Samuel 1) rep. Elizabethtown in Gen assembly in 1710, will dated 1723, m (?) and had

1. Samuel

THIRD AND FOURTH GENERATION

DANIEL MARSH 3 (John 2, Samuel 1) m Mary Rolph. They had b eleven children . John, Daniel, Henry, Christopher abt. 1743, Rolph, Ephraim, Mary, Esther, Hannah, Phebe and Rhoda

SAMUEL MARSH 3 (Joseph 2, Samuel 1) of Rahway, N. J., will dated 1771, had b

William, Dec 9, 1734

FOURTH AND FIFTH GENERATION

DANIEL MARSH 4 (Daniel 3, John 2, Samuel 1) was prob (?) the Daniel Marsh interested with John Cleves Symmes in the Miami Ohio Land Purchase If so (?) he had son Daniel, grandson Elias Morse Marsh and great grandson Robert S Marsh now in Cincinnati, O.

CHRISTOPHER MARSH 4 (Daniel 3, John 2, Samuel 1) of Rahway River, N J., d Oct 26, 1810, æ 67, m. Ann Brown, dau. George, of Scotch origin, she d Dec., 1813, æ 64 . They had b. :

1 Mary,   m. John Crowell.
2. Ephraim,   d. unm.
3 George,   m Margaret Burnwold.
4 Jennet, d. y.
5 John, b. abt 1777, "d. Nov. 1813, æ. 36," m Mary Fitz Randolph
6 Elihu, b Oct. 22, 1777, m Catherine Anderson, July 22, 1801, rem to Cincinnati, O , had 11 children, d before Feb 6, 1830
7. Jennet
8 Rolph C ,   m Deborah Hill, res Concord, Delaware Co , Pa
9 Hetty,   m Safety Layton of West Jersey
10 Robert,   m Rhoda Marsh of Staten Island, N Y

WILLIAM MARSH 4 (Samuel 3, Joseph 2, Samuel 1) m Nov 4, 1753, Sarah Webster. They had b

1 James, Sept 10, 1768, m May 24, 1792, Margaret Elston, Rahway, N J.

ALEXANDER MARSH 1, OF BRAINTREE.

ALEXANDER MARSH 1, of Braintree, now Quincy, Mass , freeman May 3. 1654, born Eng abt. 1628, m. (1) Dec 19, 1655 Mary Belcher, dau. Gregory, whose wid Catherine Belcher in her will 1680 mentions her " Mary Marsh " Alex. Marsh was rep 1692, d March 7, 1698, æ 70 He m. (2) Bathsheba, who d Jan. 8, 1723, æ. 82, says grave stone at Dorchester, Mass. Children of Alexander and Mary Marsh :

1. Mary, b Feb. 21, 1659, m Dependence French abt 1683 and had dau Mary, b. March 30, 1684, she d before 1688 and he m (2) Rebecca and had son John, b. March 10, 1689.
2. Elizabeth, b 1860.
3. Ann, b. prob (?) 1662? m Sam French and had son Samuel, " b. 1680 " prob. 1686, as next child was b in 1688
4 Katheren, b. Dec 12, 1664
5 Mercy, b April 2, 1669, bap Sept. 29, 1672, m Nov 29, 1689, Samuel Bass
6 Nathaniel, b Oct. 17, 1672
7. Rachel, b Feb 2, 1674, bap April 19, 1674, m. Mr Weston after 1698
8. Phebe, bap Sept 3, 1676, m Mr Tirrell, after 1698
9 John, b Feb 17, 1678 (or 9?) bap. March 2, 1679, m Sarah Wilson, after 1698.

SECOND AND THIRD GENERATION

JOHN MARSH 2 (Alex. 1) of Braintree, Mass now Quincy, m. Sarah Wilson, dau. Dr. John, first physician in Quincy, grandson of John Wilson the first minister of Boston. Several Wilson Marshes, his descendants, appear in different states of our Union Children, b. at Braintree :

1. John, b 1700, bap. July 25, 1703
2. Sarah, bap April 30, 1704.
3. Alexander, bap. Feb. 11, 1705, d y.
4 Alexander, bap. May, 1707.
5. Ambrose, bap June 5, 1709, d unm æ 24.
6 Wilson, bap Aug. 10, 1710
7 Moses, bap. Feb. 28, 1714
8 Samuel, June 30, 1717
9. Edmund, Sept 1, 1720, d æ. 8.
10 Mary, May 6, 1722, d y
11. Ezekiel, Aug. 13, 1724, d. y

THIRD AND FOURTH GENERATION.

JOHN MARSH 3 (John 2, Alex. 1) Grad. H. C 1726, rem to Haddam, Ct , abt 1750 and (according to Rev. Christopher Marsh) d. Nov. 7, 1755, æ. 55, Gravestone   He m 1726 or 7 Submit Woodward. Children .

1. John, bap April 23, 1728, d y
2 Elizabeth, May 4, 1729
3 John, Feb 28, 1731.
4 Edmund, April 19, 1733
5 Alice, 1736
6 Submit, Aug. 20, 1738

7 Lemuel, Aug. 9, 1741.
8 Anna, May 15, 1748
9. Sarah, prob. b. after her parents left Quincy as her name is not found in Quincy records

SARAH MARSH 3 (John 2. Alex. 1) m June 15, 1748, John Hall of Hingham, his 2d wife His 3d wife was Susannah Adams, wid of Dea. John and mother of John Adams. President of the United States. Sarah (Marsh) Hall had :

1. Lydia, who d Sept 27, 1753, æ. 2

ALEXANDER MARSH 3, of Quincy (John 2, Alex. 1) m.   He rem to Holliston, Mass about 1750 and d æ 83, abt 1790, wife d before him æ. 74. They had :

1. Hannah, bap Dec 2, 1739
2. Jerusha, bap July 5, 1741
3 Catherine, bap Sept 25, 1743.
4. Esek, b May 5, 1745

5. Amariah, Feb. 27. 1747.
6. Penelope, Feb. 26, 1748.
7. Elisha, Jan 20, 1751
8 Reuben.

WILSON MARSH 3, of Quincy (John 2, Alex 1) m. 1748 Abigail Allen, wid. Jonathan, b. May 6, 1716, dau. Experience Mayhew of Chilmark, Martha's Vineyard She d April 19, 1799, æ 83. He d. May 20, 1798, æ. 88. Children b :

1
2 } Twins, b. and d 1749.

3. Wilson, b. Aug. 10, 1750 (O. S.).

4 Jonathan, April 19, 1753, (N S)
5 Abigail, May 6, 1756.

MOSES MARSH 3, of Quincy (John 2, Alex. 1) m. Sept. 5, 1739 Sarah Crosby, dau Simon of Quincy. He was drafted and d. at Greenbush, N. Y. Wid. m. Dec 13, 1761 Wm. Hayden of Boston. Children b. .

1. Mary, April 30, 1740, d. y
2. Sarah, Dec. 13, 1741, m Sam. Peck
3 Moses, Feb 5, 1744.
4 Rachel, Aug 24, 1746, m Joseph Brackett.

5. Anna, March 5, 1749, m. —— Thomas.
6 Phebe, May 12, 1753, d unm. 1834. æ. 81
7. Mary, Nov 5 1756, m Jona. Damon

SAMUEL MARSH 3, of Braintree (John 2, Alex. 1) m. Jemima
Spear, Dec. 31, 1741, rem. in 1764 to what is now Economy, Colchester Co., Nova Scotia, with his family. They had b. :

1. Samuel, bap. Oct. 17, 1742.
2. Joshua, b. Braintree, March 16, 1745,
   bap. March 25, 1744—5.
3. Elijah, bap. Oct. 19, 1746.
4. Jemima, bap. June 5, 1748, m. Mr.
   Whitehead and had son John and
   dau. who m. in Nova Scotia. She
   and son John visited Quincy in 1801.
5. Nathaniel, b. March 29, 1750.
6. Henry, July 21, 1754.
7. John, b. March 21, 1756.
8. Josephus, b. Sept. 10, 1762, bap. Sept.
   12, 1762.

They found very rich land in Nova Scotia, but one of Samuel's
grandsons told E. J. Marsh at Portland, Me. that his grandfather
was never sorry for leaving Mass. but once, and that was from the
time he left till he died.

FOURTH AND FIFTH GENERATIONS.

ELIZABETH MARSH 4, of East Haddam, Ct. (John 3, John 2, Alex.
1) m. Israel Spencer, d. Nov. 18, 1813, had seven children :

1. Jared Wilson,
2. Israel,
3. Senelon (Fenelon?),
4. Charles,
5. Mehitabel,
6. Lucy,
7. A dau. unmarried, d. y.

JOHN MARSH 4 (John 3, John 2, Alex. 1) m. Phebe Brainard, d.
Dec. 11, 1811, æ. 80. Had :

1. John.
2 Phebe.

EDMUND MARSH 4 (John 3, John 2, Alex. 1) of Quincy, Mass. and
Haddam, Ct. rem. to Campton, N. H. 1764 and d. there Dec. 30,
1811, æ. 78, m. Eleanor Holmes, dau. Dea. Christopher of Hadlyme,
Ct. She d. Oct. 9, 1792, æ. 55. They had b. :

1. Edmund, May, 1758.
2. Christopher, d. y.
3. John, 1763.
4. Woodward.
5. Holmes.
6. Ebenezer, d. y.
7. Sylvester, 1768, m. Phebe, she d.
   April 1, 1842, æ. 79. He d. June
   22, 1794.
8. Newton, d. Compton. N. H., æ. 73.
9. Christopher, (Rev. of West Rox-
   bury, Mass.)
10. Sarah, b. 1774, m. Sam. Brooke and
    d. June 24, 1843, æ. 69.
11. Alice Wilson, d. unm. April 5, 1811,
    æ. 31.

ALICE MARSH 4 (John 3, John 2, Alex. 1) m. Dea. Jabez Comstock, d. July 27, 1818, æ. 82, he d. Oct. 7, 1807, æ. 84. They had :

1. Jabez.
2. Bela.
3. John Newton.
4. Calvin.
5. Alice.
6. Jeremiah.
7. Sarah.
8. Ann.

SUBMIT MARSH 4 (John 3, John 2, Alex. 1) m. Asa Comstock, d. July 4, 1792, æ. 53. He d. Jan. 11, 1831, æ. 100 years. They had :

1. Asa.
2. Chloe.
3. Elijah.
4. Charles.
5. Mary.
6. Submit.
7. Dorothy.
8. Silver.
9. Deborah.

LEMUEL MARSH 4, of East Haddam, Ct. (John 3, John 2. Alex. 1) m. Hannah Spencer, rem. abt. 1803 to Plainfield, Otsego Co., N. Y. and d. three or four years later. Wife d. a few years later. They had :

1. Lemuel, m. Mary Backus and moved to Ohio.
2. Samuel, m. Betty Belden, d. Genesee Co., N. Y.
3. Spencer, b. 1784, d. Albion, Mich., 1867, æ. 83. His wid. 41 years at Albion, Lovisa (Wood) Marsh was living May 13, 1885, almost 99 years of age.
4. Hannah,   d. unm. at Corning, N. Y.
5. Margaret,   m. Dyer Abbey, res. near Albany, N. Y.
6. Sarah,   m. Elnathan Hatch, d. Mad. Co., N. Y.
7. Betsey,   m. David Acley, d. near Corning, N. Y.
8. Anna,   m. John Thompson, Genesee Co., N. Y.

ANNA MARSH 4 (John 3, John 2, Alex. 1) m. Daniel Brainard of East Haddam, Ct. Had :

1. Son, d. æ. 61.
2. Hannah, b. 1770, m. Mr. Gates, living at East Haddam, a wid. in 1844.

JERUSHA MARSH 4 (Alex. 3, John 2, Alex. 1) m..—— Newton of Hopkinton, Mass., " offspring numerous," d. 1835, æ. 94.

CATHERINE MARSH 4 (Alex. 3, John 2, Alex. 1) m. Dea. Jesse Haven of Holliston, Mass. " offspring numerous " " both d. in good old age."

4

ESEK MARSH 4, (Alex. 3, John 2, Alex 1) ch mem Holliston,
Mass. 60 years, Dea. 42 years, m. Sophia Adams, b March 14,
1749, dau. Henry of Medfield. He d. Nov. 28, 1835 in 91st year of
his age His wife d April 14, 1826, æ. 77 They had b

  1 Amelia Sophia, March 10, 1776, d Jan 4
  2. Esek, March 12, 1777, m Lucinda Bullard, d April 9, 1823
  3 Lucinda, Dec 26, 1778, m Jonathan Rugg, no children
  4 Elizabeth, Nov 23, 1780, d Dec 21, 1780
  5 Alexander, Jan 3, 1782, m Catherine Ball, res Berlin and Southboro, and
        d July 1, 1845, æ. 66 1-2 years, left an only child Alexander, now aged
        80, living 1886 at Worcester, Mass
  6 Henry Adams, Oct. 11, 1783, m Clarissa Drayton Fanbanks, he d March
        18, 1833
  7 Charles, Oct 30, 1785, m Apr 6, 1808, Sally Walker, he d. Oct 28, 1845
  8 Cyrus, Oct. 30, 1787, m Mar. 28, 1816, Nancy Thayer, he d Mar 23 1878
  9 Amos, May 3, 1790, m   Olive Penniman, he d Jan. 3, 1833
  10 Betsy, Aug 15, 1792, d unm Oct 12, 1882
  11 Sarah, July 5, ———, d unm Apr 19, 1840.

AMARIAH MARSH 4 (Alex 3, John 2, Alex. 1) m. Lois Fisk abt
1768, and rem. to Pawtucket, R 1 They had b :

  1. Seneca, July 14, 1769.   5 Sylvia, unm
  2 Martin, Apr 27, 1771   6 John, d y
  3. Amariah, May 30, 1773   7 Nancy, d. unm æ 21.
  4 Betsey, m ——— Peck of Mendon   8 Lois, m Isaac Whittaker

REUBEN MARSH 4 (Alex 3, John 2, Alex. 1) had dau. Mrs. Calvin
Sparrowk, who rem and d near Black River, N. Y.

MOSES MARSH 4 (Moses 3, John 2, Alex 1) m. Jerusha Owen ;-
rem to Rockingham, Vt ("Numerous offspring ")

WILSON MARSH 4 of Quincy (Wilson 3, John 2, Alex. 1) m Susanna Savil, b May 12, 1756, dau Dr Elisha. She d June 1, 1815,
æ. 59. This Wilson, his father Wilson, and grandfather John, were
all born in the house built by his great-grandfather, Alexander 1. He
d July 7, 1828, æ 78. They had b .

  1. Elisha, July 13, 1782   5. Susannah, Aug 3, 1792
  2. Ann, June 10, 1784   6 Susannah Sept 10, 1794 (called Sarah
  3 Jonathan, Apr. 4, 1787.   until her sister d in 1697).
  4. Ambrose, Nov. 7, 1790   7. Lucretia, Jan 10, 1796.
              8. Thomas Mayhew, Aug 2, 1799

JONATHAN MARSH 4 of Quincy (Wilson 3, John 2, Alex. 1) m.
May 21, 1778. Miriam Reed of Abington, dau. Phebe (Tirrel) Reed,
whose mother, Phebe (Marsh) Tirrel, was dau. Alexander Marsh 1.
She d. May 24, 1804, æ. 47. He d. Nov. 6, 1822, æ. 70. They had:

1. John R., 1779,   } twins.
2. Abigail, 1779, m. Thomas Hayden Aug. 27, 1797, }
3. Mary.   6. Edmund, Nov. 6, 1788.
4. Moses, Jan. 29, 1785.   7. Miriam, July 22, 1792.
5. Esther, Nov. 26, 1786.   8. Wm. Mayhew, Jan. 5, 1800, d. Sept. 19, 1800.

ABIGAIL MARSH 4 (Wilson 3, John 2, Alex. 1) m. May 15, 1788,
Seth Spear, and their second child, Sophia, b. Dec. 1, 1790, m. June
13, 1811, her cousin, Jonathan Marsh 5 (Wilson 4).

SAMUEL MARSH 4 of Braintree (Samuel 3, John 2, Alex. 1) m.
(1) Apr. 14, 1764, Elizabeth Chaddrick, who d. young. He m. (2)
Elizabeth Owen, dau. Joseph. He rem. with his father to Nova
Scotia, ret. to Boston, went to Rockingham, Vt., and to Canada.
Children:

1. Louisa.   5. Nancy, m. Horace Gear, wid.
2. Elizabeth, d. y.   6. Rebecca, d. y.
3. Samuel of Whitestown, N. Y.   7. Sybel, d. y.
4. James of Woonsocket, Vt. in 1848. 8. Sally, m. Mr. Boyes.
        Windsor,

JOSHUA MARSH 4 (Samuel 3, John 2, Alex. 1) m. at Londonderry,
Nova Scotia, Mar. 24, 1770, Margaret Corbet, b. Plymouth, Mass.,
Jan. 28, 1752. He settled at Economy, Colchester Co., N. S. They
had b.:

1. Isabel, Dec. 6, 1771.   7. Samuel, Apr. 9, 1784.
2. Sarah, Sept. 26, 1773.   8. Eleanor, May 2, 1787.
3. Peleg, July 8, 1775.   9. Wilson, Apr. 21, 1789.
4. Elizabeth, Aug. 29, 1777.   10. Alexander, Apr. 21, 1791.
5. Joshua, Aug. 5, 1779.   11. Charles, Apr. 23, 1793.
6. John, May 24, 1781.   Many descendants in Wisconsin.

ELIJAH MARSH 4 (Samuel 3, John 2, Alex. 1) m. (2) Jameson (?)
Baines, mother of all his children. She d. abt. 1825, and he 1815,
in Nova Scotia. He was of Braintree, and prob. renr. to Nova Scotia
after 1801.

1. James Richardson.   5. Moses, b. in Boston, 1801.
2. John, d. y.   6. Henry, b. in Nova Scotia.
3. Ebenezer.   7. Hannah, b. in Nova Scotia.
4. Rebecca.

HENRY MARSH 4 (Samuel 3, John 2, Alex 1) m (?), settled in Otsego Co , N Y

         Who will give his descendants?

JOHN MARSH 4 (Samuel 3, John 2, Alex 1) of Economy, N S , had children ·
    1 Andrew, res Five Islands, Colchester Co , N. S
    2 Daughter, who m ——·— Thompson

JOSEPHUS MARSH 4 (Samuel 3, John 2, Alex 1) of Braintree, Mass , rem. 1664 to Economy, N S., m July 21, 1788, at Londonderry, N. S , Martha Corbet, b there Feb. 14, 1771   She d Jan 9, 1862   He d Aug. 4, 1819   They had b. :

1 William, Apr 5, 1790	8 Eleanor, Mar 5, 1804
2 Robert, Nov 20, 1791.	9 Silas, Apr. 15, 1806.
3 James, Nov 11, 1793	{ 10 Martha, Aug 9, 1808
4. Alexander, Sept 29, 1795	{ 11 Thomas, Aug 9, 1808
5. Joseph, Nov. 3, 1797	12. Mary, Aug. 13, 1811.
6 George, Jan 31, 1800.	13 Margaret, Oct. 24, 1814.
7. Agnes, Mar 3, 1802	

JOHN OF BOSTON AND HIS DESCENDANTS.

John Marsh 1, of Boston, Mass., m. Sarah ——. They had b. at Boston:

1. John, Aug. 29, 1669.
2. Joseph, Feb. 3, 1670—1.
3. Bartholomew, July 3, 1673.

SECOND GENERATION.

Joseph Marsh 2 (John 1) m. March 2, 1692—3 Ann Thurogood, married by Samuel Sewall, Esq. Asst. They had b. at Boston:

1. Joseph, Dec. 21, 1694.
2. John, Aug. 2, 1696.

THIRD GENERATION.

We next find 19 miles from Boston two brothers Joseph and John whose ages of marriage suggest their origin.

Joseph Marsh 3, of Medfield, Mass., rem. to Sturbridge called Dumer and Douglas (prob. son of Joseph 2, John 1). He had land in Douglas 1726, and house in 1746-7 and house where first town meeting was held and he a selectman, m. Sarah ——. They had b.:

1. Joseph, Dec. 22, 1718, at Medfield.
2. Keziah, Sept. 3, 1720, at Sturbridge.
3. Seth, Jan. 18,1722-3, at Sturbridge.
4. Asa, Aug. 31, 1724, at Medfield.
5. Thomas, Oct. 6, 1728, at Medfield.
6. Eli, Feb. 19, 1731, at Medfield.

John Marsh 3, of Medfield, Mass. (prob. son of Joseph 2, John 1) m. 1719 Martha Hartshorn of Dedham. They had b.:

1. John, Nov. 24, 1720, d. April 2, 1788.
2. James, Sept. 20, 1723.

Was he not the Dea. John Marsh of Douglas and he or his son the John who was the selectman and town clerk?

FOURTH GENERATION.

Joseph Marsh 4 (Joseph 3, and prob. Joseph 2, John 1) his father one of Grantees of Sturbridge rem. from Medfield to Sturbridge 1729, d. Sturbridge April 21, 1800, m. Abigail ——. They had b.:

1. Sarah, April 2, 1748.
2. Chloe, Aug. 28, 1750.
3. Marian, June 22, 1752.
4. Abibail, Jan 23, 1754
5. Joseph, Dec. 26, 1755.
6. Keziah, July 18, 1757.

7. Sibel, Mar 31, 1759.
8 Jaspei, Aug 17, 1760.
9 Caroline, Feb 2, 1762.
10 Judith, July 28, 1764   She m. Henry
      Morse, Jan. 7, 1790
11 Catherine, Mar 28, 1767

12 Hinsdell, Dec 8, 1768

SETH MARSH 4 of Douglas, Mass (Joseph 3, and prob. Joseph 2, John 1) m Feb 27, 1749-50, Rachel Ellis of Douglas They had b. :

1. Aaron, July 26, 1751.
2. Rachel, Dec. 30, 1753
3. Sarah, Feb. 13, 1755 } (?)
4. Sarah, Feb 13, 1756 }

5 Nathan, May 2, 1758.
6 Oliver, Mar 13, 1760 (d May 12, 1774)
7 Esther, May 24, 1762.
8. Obed, July 10, 1764

ASA MARSH 4 of Douglas and Whately (Joseph 3, and prob Joseph 2, John 1), a nail-maker, rem. to Whately 1783, d 1802 (?), m abt 1749, Melissa Wheeler or " Millicent Woodstock" (?) They had b , prob. all at Douglas :

1. Jonathan, 1750,   m Hannah Balcom, had 8 children, and he d. 1827.
2. Amos,   m abt 1777, Elizabeth Jefferson, and had thirteen children
3. Asa,   1759,   m May 20, 1778, Sarah Snow, and had six children
4 Abijah,   m abt 1783, Bathsheba Snow, and had five children.
5. Sarah,   m. abt 1784, Amos Jefferson, and had four children.
6. Abner, July 21, 1763, m Mar. 6, 1788, Dorothy Dana, and had 10 children

Of THOMAS MARSH 4 (Joseph 3, prob Joseph 2, John 1) we have no trace. Who can help us?

ELI MARSH 4 of Douglas (Joseph 3, prob. Joseph 2, John 1) m. Mary ———. They had b :

1. Aaron, Feb 26, 1759, d Apr 29, 1807, m abt. 1777, had seven children. His wife Sarah, b. Sept. 7, 1762, d Apr 28, 1849
2. Ede, Aug. 3, 1761. 3. Eunice, Sept. 18, 1763. 4 Elisha, July 7, 1765.
          5. Ezra, Sept 27, 1767

JOHN MARSH 4 of Medfield and prob. Douglas (John 3, prob Joseph 2, John 1) m. Feb. 27, 174 (3 or 4?), Lydia Smith, who d Oct , 1803. He d Apr. 2, 1888? They had b. :

1. Sybell, May 23, 1744, m Apr , 1765, Nathan Howard
2. Lydia,   1746, d y.
3. Silas, May 13, 1747, m. (1) Feb. 8, 1775, Beulah Albee, m. (2) June 12, 1778, Deliverance Fish.

4. John, Mar. 9, 1749, m (1) May 5, 1774, Hannah Clark, m. (2) Apr 17, 1780, Levina Gibbs He d Aug 30, 1820
5. Duty, Jan 13, 1750, m Mar 27, 1781, Rhoda Morse
6 Lydia, Oct 30, 1752, m Oct 19, 1773, Luke Harding
7 Martha, Apr 17, 1755, m Stephen Harding
8 Calvin, Mar 14, 1757
9 Anna, Oct 5, 1758
10 Mary, Dec. 10, 1760
11. Molly, Sept 17, 1763, m Aug 30, 1786, John Plympton, son of Col Daniel. She d Medfield, Sept 20, 1840
12 Ichabod, Oct 16, 1764
13 Silence, June 15, 1766
14. Amy, m Jan 17, 1782, Jonathan Dix of Whittingham, Vt, and d. Jan 26, 1846.

Of JAMES MARSH 4 b Medfield and later prob. of Douglas (John 3, prob Joseph 2, John 1) no certain trace. Was he *possibly* father of ·

1 James Marsh, b. Douglas, Mass, Oct 21, 1751, m Mary of Acton, Mass.? or of 2 Lois Marsh, b. Douglas, Mass, Jan. 13, 1768? or of 3. Ebenezer Marsh, b Douglas, Mass, abt. 1767, (?) m. Acsah Stern? Who can tell?

WILLIAM MARSH OF PLAINFIELD, CT., AND FOUR GENERATIONS OF HIS DESCENDANTS.

In the History of the First Church, Stonington, Ct., we find the following records

"Elizabeth, wife Wm. Marsh, admitted to ch Aug 24, 1690
"Wm Marsh admitted to ch May 14, 1693
                    "CHILDREN BAPTIZED
"Sept. 7, 1690, Mary, William, Thomas, and James.
"June 19, 1692, Elizabeth.
"June 24, 1694, Ann"

We have statements that of these children William d at Plainfield, Ct., Jan. 23, 1759, æ 74. He was then b. abt. 1685, and Thomas has on tombstone "d Mar 19, 1753, in his 67th yr", therefore b. 1687, and, taking the children in the order of their names on ch record, we have:

WILLIAM MARSH 1 (brother of James who was beheaded in Eng) of Stonington, was in the Narragansett Swamp fight of 1675, m Elizabeth Yeomans of Stonington, prob abt. 1682 (?) They had b

1 Mary, abt. 1683 (?).
2 William, abt 1685
3. Thomas, abt. 1687.
4. James, abt. 1690

5 Elizabeth, abt. 1692, m. Mr Utley, and lived in ' Canada Parish," Windham, Ct
6. Ann, abt. 1694.

7 Matthias, 1695 or later
Perhaps 8 (?) Joseph, who was at Voluntown with James, 1725

The name of Matthias does not appear on Stonington church records, making it probable that William, 1 took his family to Plainfield after Elizabeth and before Matthias was born, say 1694 to 1695, although he explored there with Eld. Yeomans abt. 1690

SECOND AND THIRD GENERATIONS

WILLIAM 2 (Wm. 1) seems to have remained in Plainfield, Ct., and was in French war, 1756-7

JOSEPH (?) and James 2 (Wm 1) were at Voluntown in 1725 Who can tell us something of their descendants?

THOMAS MARSH 2 (Wm. 1) was deacon of church at Canada Parish, Windham, afterwards called Hampton, in 1730 and 1738, preached at Mansfield, Ct., where he was pastor-elect of "Separatist Ch.," was imprisoned Jan., 1746, for preaching without a license, but ordained there same year, 1746. He m. (?) Eliza ——, and they had b. :

1. Thomas, Jan. 24, 1713.
2. John, Dec. 11, 1715.
3. Elihu, July 12, 1717.
4. Amos, June 7, 1719.
5. Joseph, Apr. 9, 1721.
6. Eunice, Feb. 17, 1724.
7. William, Dec. 23, 1725.
8. Phineas, Dec. 16, 1727.
9. Simeon, Jan. 15, 1729.
10. Hannah, Oct. 17, 1730.
11. Jacob, Aug. 19, 1733.
12. Matthias, Sept. 25, 1736.

MATTHIAS 2 (Wm. 1) of Coventry. Ct., m. —— Brigham, rem. first to Dover, Dutchess Co., N. Y., where he held large tracts of land, thence removed to Dorset. Vt. They had b.:

1. William.

THIRD AND FOURTH GENERATIONS.

JOHN 3 (Thomas 2, Wm. 1) of Windham. Ct., m. (1) Sept. 25, 1736, Sarah Martin. They had b. :

1. Phineas, June 29, 1737.
2. Esther, Sept. 10, 1738.
3. Sarah, Mar. 20, 1740.
4. Lucy, Apr. 9, 1742.
5. Susannah, Dec. 2, 1743.

With some question, I add, he seems to be the John of New Milford (Ct.) History, who, perhaps, (2) (?) " m. Mary ——, settled at Dover, N. Y., and he and wife d. before 1765. Children :

"John, Abraham; Sarah m. Dan. Lake; Susanna m. Agrippa Martin; Mary, and Hannah."

ELIHU MARSH 3 (Thos. 2, Wm. 1) of Mansfield and Fairfield, Ct., commonly called, as minister, " Elder Elihu," m. Savial Abbey, d. in Fairfield, where he was living Sept. 30, 1765, when he bought his first land in New Milford, Ct. Old records say : " Marsh, Elihu, m. Zeruiah Abbe, May 10, 1736. Issue : Elihu, Jun., b. Sept. 17, 1737." They had b. :

1. Elihu, Sept. 17, 1737.
2. Saravial, May 8, 1740.
3. Mary, June 12, 1742.
4. Eunice, Dec. 6, 1744.
5. Lydia, Apr. 11, 1747.
6. John, Aug. 4, 1749.
7. Samuel, Oct. 8, 1752.
8. Joseph, Apr. 20, 1754.
9. Hannah, Feb. 20, 1757.
10. Ruth, Aug. 31, 1759.
11. Benjamin D., May 10, 1762.
12. Amos, Sept. 8, 1764.

5

Amos Marsh 3 and Jacob Marsh 3 (Thos 2, Wm 1) appear in Clarendon, Vt in 1773, also with nephews Daniel and William at Clarendon in 1769 then called, as part of New York, Socialburg An Abram Marsh called "the ablest *Yorker*," "driven from Shaftsbury" by Vermonters, was prob. the Abraham of Dover, N Y son of John 3 (Thos. 2, Wm. 1)

Hannah Marsh 3 (Thos 2, Wm. 1) m May 22, 1751, Rev. Eliphalet Wright, had nine children and d. at Hinsdale, Mass Jan 2, 1815

Joseph Marsh 3 (Thos 2, Wm. 1) was still in Canada Parish, Windham in 1763, "threaded his way from Canterbury, Ct. by marked trees" to Worthington, Mass where he was selectman 1771. 1772 and 1777, served in Rev war, prob? rem with his younger sons to Hinesburg, Vt in 1788 He m. (1) April 29, 1743 Anna Stedman, b 1729, dau. Dea. Thos and Anna. They had b.

    1 Daniel, April 5, 1744, bap April 8, d. April 26, 1753, æ. 9 years, 2 months and 21 days

    2 Anna, Nov 14, 1745, bap. Dec 15, m April 25, 1765, Eleazer Wright and had twelve children.

    3. Joseph, Dec 20, 1747,   d June 11, 1753

    4 Elizabeth, Dec 5, 1749,   d April 29, 1753.

    5 Stephen, Feb 5, 1752,   d May 8 1753

Wife Anna d April 19. 1753, æ abt 24 He m. (2) Lydia Bennett, June 20, 1754 They had b .

1. Ebenezer, Aug. 1 1755	5 Daniel, April 3, 1764.
2 Joseph, Feb. 11, 1759	6 Thomas, Dec 28, 1765
3 Rufus, Sept. 29, 1760	7 Wm B., b Windham, Ct, May 23, 1769
4 Lois, April 15, 1762.	

Col. Wm. Marsh 3 (Matthias 2, Wm. 1) of Manchester and Dorset, Vt was prominent in Revolution, on Com 1777 to consult with commander at Ticonderoga, m (?) had b :

1. Matthias.	4 Jeremiah
2 Samuel	5. William
3 Benjamin.	6 Archibald.
Also five daughters.	

Ver Hist speaks of "Johnson Marsh son Col Wm" We want dates

FOURTH AND FIFTH GENERATION.

JOHN MARSH 4 (prob. of John 3, Thos. 2, Wm. 1) of New Milford, m. Feb. 14, 1771 Rachel Prindle of New Milford, Ct. They had b. :

1. Esther, Dec. 24, 1771.
2. Lois, Oct. 23, 1773.
3. Phineas, Jan. 30, 1776.
4. Lucy, March 13, 1778.
5. Abraham, July 9, 1780.

ELIHU MARSH 4 (Elder Elihu 3, Thos. 2, Wm. 1) res. and d. in Sherman, Ct., m. Martha Waters, had b. :

1. Anna, m Enos Peck.
2. Rachel, m. Ebenezer Wright.

MARY MARSH 4 (dau. Elder Elihu) m. Ebenezer Leach, res. Sherman, Ct.

EUNICE MARSH 4 (dau. Elder Elihu) m. Joel Northrup.

LYDIA MARSH 4 (dau. Elder Elihu) m. Isaac Northrup.

RUTH MARSH 4 (dau. Elder Elihu) m. Ichabod Leach, res. Sherman, Ct.

JOHN MARSH 4 (Elihu 3, Thos. 2, Wm. 1) rem. from New Milford, Ct. to Vergennes, Vt., m. Abigail Wanzer. They had b. :

1. Polly, m. Daniel Buckley.
2. Elihu, m. Urania Stilson.
3. Wanzer, m. Sally Buckley, dau. Parsons Buckley of Danbury.
4. Reed, d. in Vergennes.
5. Daniel, m. —— Swift.
6. Vina, m. Gesham Buckley.

SAMUEL MARSH 4 (Elihu 3, Thos. 2, Wm. 1) of New Milford, m. Nov. 15, 1771, Miriam (?) or Maryann (?) Leach, she d. May 14, 1822, æ. 70. They had b. :

1. Elihu, July 7, 1773, d. y.
2. Lucinda, Aug. 15, 1774.
3. Elihu, June 9, 1776.
4. Joseph, March 16, 1778.
5. Bradley, April 23, 1780.
6. Eunice, July 1, 1782.
7. Amos Horace, March 23, 1783.
8. Lucy, March 17, 1785, d. y.
9. Susannah, Nov. 17, 1786.
10. Geo. Martin, May 12, 1789, m. Betsey Sherwood
11. Samuel Davis, Oct. 22, 1792.
12. John, July 19, 1795.

JOSEPH MARSH 4 (Elihu 3, Thos. 2, Wm. 1) of New Milford, Ct., m. (1) Nov. 29, 1781, Abigail Waldo, who d. Jan. 28, 1793. He m. (2) Deborah Waldo, Nov. 19, 1793. Children b. :

1. William, Jan 25, 1783
2. Hannah, Sept. 10, 1784, m Zachariah Ferris
3 Saravial, April 3, (?) 1787.
4 Arabella, Feb 20, 1789, m Elihu Hoag of So. Dover

5 Samuel Waldo, April 18, 1791, rem. to Ill
6 Allen, June 8, 1797
7 Abigail, Aug. 18, 1799
8 Holmon, April 28, 1802.

HON AMOS MARSH 4 (Elihu 3, Thos 2, Wm 1) m Abigail Sutton of Canaan, Ct, taught "Clio Hall" Bennington, Vt, rem to Vergennes, Vt and d Jan 4, 1811 Wid. Abigail d New Milford, Oct 11, 1844 Washington appointed Hon Amos, attorney of Vt in 1794. They had b

1 Laura, Sept 8, 1792, m Daniel Merwin of New Milford.
2 Almira, Aug 15, 1794, m Anaan Hine of New Milford

BEN D MARSH 4 (Elihu 3, Thos 2, Wm. 1) of New Milford, rem. to Bennington, Vt, m. Anna Jagger. They had b ·

1. Stephen, Aug. 19, 1795.
2 Daniel, Nov 20, 1796.
3. James, May 28, 1798
4 Eliza, June 16, 1801
5 Amos, May 22, 1803

6 Edward, Oct 5, 1804
7 Jacob, Oct 21, 1806
8 Ann M, June 13, 1808
9 Melancthon, Feb 11, 1811

JOSEPH MARSH 4 (Joseph 3, Thos. 2, Wm 1) seems to have been selectman in Worthington, Mass in 1800 and 1818 Who can give us any further trace? He or his father served in Rev war.

RUFUS MARSH 4 (Joseph 3, Thos 2, Wm. 1) Selectman at Worthington, Mass 1793. 1796 and 1797 and also Dea after his father's death or rem perhaps (?) appears with first settlers of Middlebury, Vt

DANIEL MARSH 4 (Joseph 3, Thos 2, Wm. 1) went from Worthington, Mass to Hinesburg, Vt and d. there 1838, æ. 74. Wife d. æ 85 They had son

Hon Joseph Marsh, who had son Daniel who d. 1838, æ 79

THOMAS MARSH 4 (Joseph 3, Thos 2, Wm 1) of Windham, Ct., Worthington, Mass, Hinesburg, Vt, rem to Ferrisburg, Vt What descendants?

DR WILLIAM B MARSH 4 (Joseph 3, Thos 2, Wm 1) studied with Dr Starkweather of Worthington, Mass 1792, went 1788, æ

19 to Hinesburg, Vt. and m. 1792 (?) Esther Holcomb who was of the traveling party. He d. Dec. 22, 1827 æ. 58. A representative three times.

Had a daughter Mrs. Goodyear.

MATTHIAS MARSH 4 (Col. Wm. 3, Matthias 2, Wm. 1) of Dorset, Vt. Had b. five sons:

William.	Abraham.
Edmund.	Henry.
Samuel.	

A son of Abraham is W. H. Marsh, 237 Broadway, N. Y.

DANIEL MARSH 4 (nephew Amos 3, therefore grandson Thos. 2, Wm. 1) of Clarendon, Vt., m. Mary ——. He d. Jan. 29, 1857, æ. 80, (b. abt. 1777) Mary his wife d. Feb. 1, æ. 75. They were parents of :

1. Hon. John L. Marsh of Vt. State Senate.
2. Hon. Rodney V. Marsh of Vt. House of Rep., b. July 11, 1807, m. Eliza E. Sprague. He d. March 8, 1872.

REV. CYRUS MARSH of Kent, Ct. Y. C. 1739, of Plainfield, Ct. was prob. (?) son of (Wm. 2, Wm. 1). So perhaps Isaac? Who can tell?

APPENDIX.

[By the kindness of a friend we are allowed to add, *without any expense*, the following account of our late reunion]

MARSH FAMILY REUNION.

LAKE PLEASANT, July 22d, 1886.

The three days' reunion of the Marsh family which was begun here Tuesday, ended to-day The interest has been fervent and those who have attended depart well pleased to have met and exchanged family greetings

There were representatives from New England, New York and other states, including Col. Lucius B Marsh of Boston, Josiah D Marsh of Hadley, John E Marsh of Hartford, Riverius Marsh of New Brunswick, N. J., Horatio N. Marsh of Joliet, Ill., James Marsh of Peabody, E. J. Marsh of Leominster, Mass , the president Rev. D W. Marsh of Amherst, Munsn Marsh of Belmont, Mass., the venerable Simeon B Marsh of Spencer, and others

The gathering was the means of cementing much good feeling among Marshmen and was enjoyed by all The exercises Tuesday morning opened with prayer by Rev D W Marsh of Amherst, and the report of Secretary J Johnson was accepted together with the report of Mr R. Marsh, chairman of the finance committee J Dwight Marsh in his address produced a quaint historical document of particular interest to this growing family, which now numbers over 10,000 in this country, the will of John Marsh, who came from Hartford and took up his abode in Hadley.

Particular emphasis was laid on the fact that between 1633 and 1700 various branches started in this country, viz.: From John of Salem, John of Boston, John of Hartford, Alexander of Braintree, George of Hingham, William of Plainfield and Samuel of New Haven, all of whom have left large families of descendants, many of whom are well known A book has been prepared by E J Marsh of the family of George of Hingham, which is now in press John E. Marsh

of Hartford, and E. J. Marsh of Leominster gave a few family reminiscences. It was voted to give the gathering the dignity of a name, and it will be known hereafter as the Marsh Family Association.

A committee of arrangements was appointed with Mr. D. C. Marsh as chairman, and the meeting then adjourned for dinner.

At 1.30 P. M. the family reassembled and several selections were sung from Gospel Hymns, and an original ode, to the tune "America," after which the president, Rev. D. W. Marsh of Amherst, Mass., made a brief address of welcome. In these remarks he stated that last year one of the family had presented a record box of rosewood for use in filing away letters and records pertaining to various branches of the family, and that this year it was full of a mass of valuable historical and biographical matter, and that another would soon be needed. He then read various papers and letters from the box relating to John Marsh of Salem and his descendants, George Marsh of Hingham and his descendants, Alexander Marsh of Braintree, Mass., and descendants of John Marsh of Boston, Wm. Marsh of Plainfield, Ct., and also a bundle of papers in regard to the Montague Marshes, who are descendants of John Marsh of Hartford, Ct.

The principal address of the day was by J. D. Marsh of Hadley, which in the main was an historical and biographical review of John Marsh of Hartford and Hadley. It was an interesting paper and a valuable contribution to the records of the family.

Remarks were then made by Horatio J. Marsh of Joliet, Ill., and by Riverius Marsh of New Brunswick, N. J. A letter was read from Edward Stewart of New York.

Wednesday forenoon Col. Lucius B. Marsh of Boston delivered an exhaustive and valuable address giving the early history of Salem and the genealogy of John Marsh who landed there in 1633. He corrected some errors in dates and gave an outline of the various branches of the family tree. He exhibited some of the commissions issued by the kings of England to his ancestors. The address was highly appreciated by the company present, the most of whom are eager seekers after the early history of the Marsh family. A vote of thanks was given the speaker.

The rest of the day was taken up with discussing various matters of business. A resolution from the committee of finance and publication was adopted, the gist of which was that money should be raised at once for the publication of an outline of the different

branches, and that a copy of the publication be sent to every member of the Family Association

These officers were chosen: President, Rev. Dr D W Marsh of Amherst; vice-presidents, Wm. T. Marsh, Litchfield, Ct., Chas E Marsh, New Milford, Ct , John E Marsh, Hartford, Ct , David C. Marsh, Montague, L B Marsh, Boston, Riverius Marsh, New Brunswick, N J , H N Marsh, Joliet, Ill., James Marsh, Cleveland, O , Luther R. Marsh, New York City, secretary, Jonathan Johnson. Greenfield, treasurer, E B Marsh, Amherst   It was decided to hold the next meeting at Hartford about August 1st of next year. and the president, secretary and R Marsh were appointed as the committee of arrangements   On this day and the day following several short addresses were made of much interest to those present. those participating being Riverius Marsh, E J. Marsh, Lucius B Marsh, J. Johnson and others   Letters were also read from several who were unable to attend but who felt a great interest in the work that is being undertaken of unearthing the early history of their ancestors.

ADDRESS OF J. DWIGHT MARSH OF HADLEY

Mr President, and ladies and gentlemen, I am asked to speak from Old Hadley   I am a resident of that town, and my ancestors, the *fathers*, back to the John Marsh who married Anne Webster, have all been residents of Hadley   I say the John Marsh who married Anne Webster, because, while I have found a great many John Marshs, I have found but one who married Anne Webster.   And of the *mothers* all but one have been descendants of the first settlers of Hadley.   As for several years after the town was settled no one was admitted as an inhabitant without vote of the town, whether a man was allowed to go *out of* town for a wife without leave, I do not know , but to make it right for the future generations her husband records on her tombstone in brackets that she was " descended from pious parents", who they were I do not know. This was the mother of the Rev Elisha, of whom we heard last year.

In my house I have a picture representing Hadley attacked by the Indians in 1675, and the majestic figure of Goffe standing in the foreground rallying the panic stricken inhabitants   But, says the historian of to-day, " all tradition , no Indians nearer Hadley than Deerfield that day "   I have looked at the records of the town of that time and find that it was a time of great trouble for fear of the

enemy, as they call them. Votes were passed that the fortifications be strengthened ; brush be cut down in all home lots, so as not to be a hiding place for the enemy ; that no less than 40, or more than 50, men should go outside the fortifications to gather the crops in the meadows, and they should dispose themselves in the best manner for protection ; that all males over 16 go armed to church, etc. A garrison was kept there in the winter of 1675 and summer of 1676. Had the Indians been successful, as at Deerfield, and Goffe been tomahawked, there would have been no need of secresy, but I notice that Goffe was on the winning side, whether as one of the judges of Charles 1st, or in a sword contest in Boston or New Haven, or fighting the Indians in Hadley ; and to have published the story at that time would have been *death* to protectors as well as the protected. Now Peter Tilton, one of the protectors, was a very modest man, and would naturally object to that way of being taken off. I notice that in recording the list of Selectmen for the town, while giving every other man his full title as Capt., Lieut., Sergt., Cornet, etc., he would write his own name last, and simply as P. T., although entitled to more titles than any other man in town.

The Rev. Samuel Hopkins, writing in 1793 to President Stiles of New Haven, speaks of the tradition in the family of the Marshs ; John Marsh being one of the Selectmen in 1675, would know the facts in the case, and thus very likely the tradition would be handed down in the family. And President Stiles speaks of meeting in Wethersfield a Mrs. Porter, a sensible and judicious woman, a daughter of Mr. Ebenezer Marsh, born next door to Peter Tilton's, and of her story in relation to the judges. Thus the Marshs are brought in for their share in these traditions.

Another historical fact in which I took some interest was the passing of Burgoyne's army through the town, and while here Burgoyne presenting a sword to Gen. Porter. I saw in a Springfield paper this summer that the army passed through Springfield. Springfield had her Bay path, but Hadley had also her Bay road, and both led to Boston. Now in this instance no one's life was in danger, if the truth were known, and I have been fortunate in having a chance to look over a diary, kept in Hadley from 1740 to 1780, not indeed by a Marsh but by one whose descendants are entitled to a place in this gathering, as his wife was Miriam Cook, the daughter of Lieut. Samuel Cook and Ann, daughter of Jonathan Marsh. In it he says, " Oct. 22, 1777, William returns home from the taking of Burgoyne

6

with 5200 men, near Fort Edward." "Oct. 29, prisoners pass this
week; viz., about half Burgoyne's army taken at Saratoga by Gen
Gates;" "Nov 8th, one of the prisoners passing dies in this town ,"
"10th another prisoner dies " He speaks of noises heard thus :
"thunder, like guns," and "July 5th, 1777, a noise like cannon
heard, whether thunder or not " We have doubtless all heard of the
dark day about this time, in which people were greatly frightened,
and it is said one old lady exclaimed " Oh dear, the day of judgment
is come, and Elly is off in the northern army without a nutcake in
his pocket," and as she could not help him she would do what she
could and she calls to Betty to get the geese in, and having made all
snug she bides her time   On her monument I read,

> When the last trumpet sounds,
> Arise, come forth ye dead,
> Shall be the call to her and all
> That sleep in cozy beds "

I have the old family Bible in my possession, and its well thumbed
pages attest that it was not kept as a parlor ornament   Another
question in which the Marsh family are interested is, Did John Marsh
stay in Old Hadley? Says the Hadley History. John Marsh was
one of the first settlers of Hadley, but removed thence, first to Northampton,* and then to Hartford, where he died in 1688   The first
notice of John Marsh, which I find in the Hadley records, is at the
first town meeting held at Warner's house, Oct. 8th, 1660, "Agreed
that Jo Marsh hath his house lot with his father, Mr Webster, of
Mr. Webster's, and he to have eight acres allowed for it within the
fence, and he to come up at spring next " They had cast lots for
their land in Feb of 1660, and Mr Webster drew No. 19, and John
Marsh No 31 I think he came up in 1661, as in December John
Marsh and Will Webster engage for Robt Webster. He has his
lands recorded the 19th of June, 1674, as John Marsh, Sen., and as
the third John was born in 1668 there were three generations of that
name, probably, in town in 1674   In 1675, John Marsh was one of
the Selectmen, whether senior or junior I do not know. This is the
only time I find his name as a town officer, while the names of his
sons, Jonathan and Daniel, recorded first as Jonathan and Daniel
and then as Lieut. Jonathan and Sergt. Daniel, and lastly as Mr ,
which title they have on their tombstones, are on every page of

---

* It is an interesting fact that in the record of original members of the first church in
Northampton formed in 1661 the name of John Marsh is the second on the list   But Hadley
and Northampton are only three miles apart   D W M

Hadley History from 1682 to 1715. The next time I find John
Marsh's name is in the Probate office at Northampton, March 3d,
1687.

"A true copy of the last will and testament of John Marsh of Hadley, who dyed
at Windsor, presented at the Court at Northampton, the 4th of December, 1688.

I, John Marsh, of Hadley, in the county of Hampshire, in New England, being
very sensible of mine own frailty and mortality, yet through the mercy of God, of
sound mind and memory at present, doe make this my last will and Testament as
follows: I commit my selfe soule and body into the hands of the Almighty and
Eternal God whose I am, and into the arms of my Redeemer the Lord Jesus Christ,
in whom I desire steadfastly to belong, and on whom do repose and rest alone for
righteousness life and salvation, leaving my body to be interred with a comely
burial.

And for the outward estate the Lord hath blessed me withal, my will is, that
after my just debts are paid, and funeral expenses discharged, that then

I give to my son, John Marsh, ffive pounds.

I give to my son, Jonathan Marsh, all my Gold.

I give to my son, Daniel Marsh, my two Cob Irons.

I give to my daughter, Hannah Loomis, alias Marsh, thirty pounds, unless I
pay a part of it before my decease, n'th, if so then so much shall be discounted
from the Legacy.

I give to my son, Samuel Marsh all my lands within the township of Hadley.

I give to my daughter, Lydia Marsh, my green Ring.

I give to my grandson Baker, of Northampton, ffive pounds, when he shall
attayne to the age of one and twenty years

I give and bequeath to my daughter, Lydia Marsh, twenty pounds.

And all said Legacies, my will is, that my Executors see faithfully discharged.
And I do constitute and appoint my loving sons, John Marsh and Samuel Marsh,
to be Executors to this my will annulling and making voide all former wills at any
time by me willed or bequeathed.

JOHN MARSH.

Sealed and subscribed in the presence of

THOMAS HOVEY,
THOMAS HEAD."

You see, Mr. President, that our ancestor Daniel was remembered
in the will; how valuable the two cob irons were, or what has become
of them I do not know. I have tried to find out what kind of houses
those first settlers built. I find a vote March 6th, '64–'65: "The
town have ordered that every inhabitant of this town shall provide
and maintain a sufficient ladder that shall reach to the top of his
dwelling house, and another, or two, which, being joined together,
shall reach to the top of the barn." So that the houses were not as
high as the barns. The first meeting house was a barn-like structure
lasting about fifty years. The first school house to be 18x25 feet,

and 7 feet betwixt joints   The oldest house now standing in town was built in 1713, and is what I call the second crop of houses These show good workmanship, and were of two stories, about 20x40 feet, divided into three parts, containing two rooms and a chimney   I never heard that the fireplace was not large enough for the wood, but have heard that the wood was too large for the door of the house   Nearly all the houses built in the first half of the 18th century were of this plan   The house in Middle street, which stood where the present Town Hall stands, and said to have been the first house built in the street, was built by a Marsh.   This house stood till 1811, so that I well recollect its second story projecting over the first   The lot was granted to Daniel Marsh in 1686, the house not built until 1713   The old diary to which I have referred, was kept by the owner of this house, and I find these entries in it " 1713, Feb 28   This day I received deed of Home lot of Mr. Marsh, at 3.30£ , May 17, 1713, Mr Marsh moved out of my house "   This house when first built had small windows of diamond glass, of which I have one light, not a quality which would pass for No 1 in these days   The cellar was only under one room, and the owner makes record at one time that he has 16 barrels of cider in cellar, 8 of which in rum casks, stand on the north side of cellar   It may have been a short crop, for I find he buys 111 gallons of rum at one time the same year.

The old Marsh house which stood on the Stanley Porter lot was used as a tavern at the time of the Revolution, and a Tory lodged there and the boys tried to smoke him out by covering the top of the chimney, but there was a Hannah there who made them remove it, and protected her guest   In a list of thirty-three families descended from John Marsh, which I have, I find seventeen Hannahs   The three Daniels in town, who married, each took a Hannah for a wife   The longest-lived Marsh was a Daniel, who never married The next, Joseph, had four wives and outlived them all

As the old Marsh lot from 1660 had been known by the name of John, so near the last it had three owners by the name of Ebenezer, the last occupant, an Ebenezer, dying a bachelor.   The property was divided among his brother's children, and by one of them the old house was torn down in 1821, and the lot sold out of the family

On two ridges of ground west of the street, is the old cemetery, swept by the fierce blasts of winter, as one writing to me from the west well knew, who had nothing better to give me an idea of the

prairie winds than to say, they cut as they do on Hadley meadows. On the west knoll, and midway from north to south in the yard, stands the monument of Daniel Marsh, and those of his sons John, Job, William, and of the two wives of his son Ebenezer, and of children's children to the fourth generation, twenty-four in all; and doubtless a great many unmarked graves. On one stone I read: " Let not the dead forgotten lie, lest living men forget to die "—a text on stone, its audience stones, for they have lain this many a year forgotten and unknown. The monuments to Jonathan and Dorcas, his wife, stand alone in another part of the yard. He had but one son, the Rev. Jonathan, who was probably buried at Windsor, Ct., where he was settled for life. A vast number, scattered far and near, can trace their ancestry back to Jonathan Marsh through his five daughters and their 34 children, and of course far more to John his father, the first Marsh of Hadley.

ADDRESS OF COL. LUCIUS B. MARSH OF BOSTON.

In introducing Col. Marsh, who had been for thirty-eight years a successful merchant in Boston, retiring a few years since, the President particularly requested him to give some account of his military experience and defence of New Orleans during the war, but he modestly omitted it. The editor therefore condenses here a few facts from the Adjutant General's report for 1863.

" The 47th Regiment was recruited chiefly by Lucius B. Marsh, Esq., a well known and respected merchant of Boston, who was elected and commissioned as colonel. The regiment was a part of Gen. Banks' Secret Expedition, a portion of which was under the Col's command and left New York Dec. 22, 1862; sailing under sealed orders, to be opened at sea.

After commanding other posts in defence of New Orleans, La., the Col. was ordered on the 19th of May by Gen. T. W. Sherman to Camp Parapet (the chief defense), to encamp there and assume command of the United States forces stationed there, consisting of portions of the 12th Maine, 4th Wisconsin, 128th New York, 15th New Hampshire, 26th Connecticut, 6th Michigan, and 12th Massachusetts Batteries, Companies B. and C., 1st Regiment H. A. N. Native Guards, two companies 42d Massachusetts, two companies Metropolitan Cavalry, also, temporarily, the 1st Texas Cavalry, and 1st Regiment Engineers Native Guards. The Colonel recruited a company of colored men to be used in the swamps, which became the nucleus of the 2d Regiment of Engineers.

The line of defences was about thirty miles   The immediate
defences consisted of the Parapet two and a-half miles long, situated
on the east side of the river, running from the Mississippi to the
swamps and Lake Ponchartrain, and on the west side of the river
Fort Banks, and there was a canal and military road to be guarded
and scouted, a distance of twelve to seventeen miles through the
swamps to the Lake

"With a large force of Confederates in front of these defences,
this important post was held under peculiar circumstances during
the siege of Port Hudson."

The smaller force *checkmated* the larger, and thus New Orleans
was kept safe

Gen Sherman made particular mention " of the 47th and its colonel for marked ability" and Gen Banks was " certain that these
arduous sacrifices and honorable triumphs would not be forgotten
by the country or the government they helped to preserve."

The second days' session opened with music and the address of the
day was made by Hon. Lucius B Marsh of Boston and follows :

Mr. President, Ladies and Gentlemen —

Tradition says, that soon after the Battle of Hastings, William the
Conqueror made an extended tour through a great portion of England, accompanied by a brilliant staff of both military officers and confidential friends.   They followed the roads made long before with much
skill and labor by the Romans which now sadly needed repairs   The
culverts were many of them out of order, and thus the king's high-
way " so-called " had formed dams which caused small lakes and
ponds of water, which covered the low lands and extended moors.
Water and wet lands made up quite a portion of the landscape.   As
they passed through the country, William's attention was called to
these overflowed, low and unproductive lands   It was suggested to
him that a comprehensive system of drainage would cure the evil,
and make the moors the most productive and valuable lands in the
kingdom   This matter of drainage was quite a new thing, the old
system was to keep the water from coming in and, " this was to draw
the water off and dispose of it "   To this far seeing and confidential
friend of his staff, William, intrusted this important work   Without
going farther into detail, I would say, that this man wherever he
went in his official capacity, was known as the Marsh man ; and that he
showed capacity sufficient to accomplish this great work of internal
improvement in England there is no doubt

The very best lands, the most productive, and the most valuable, and the beautiful landscapes, the verdant fields and lovely valleys, that call forth such admiration from the travelers as the swiftly passing train takes him on his journey! Can one believe that these now so beautiful, were once the moors, the bogs, the constantly wet low lands of no value, but unhealthy as well as unsightly? All this change was accomplished by the brain work of William the Conquerer's confidential friend and his successors, who became known throughout the realm, as the Marsh man, and finally by the name of Marsh. Did we originate from this man? I cannot say. If so, I am not ashamed of our ancestor.

Tradition says that three or four brothers came from England early in the 17th century, about 1630, by the name of Marsh. One settled in Salem, one in Hingham, one in Connecticut, and accounts of the fourth differ, some thinking that he returned to England. Our historians here present agree that this cannot be true as to the brotherhood.

I think, however, that though not true strictly to the letter, still there is something in it. Certainly three young men by the name of Marsh did come from England to this country, one, John, from whom the speaker descended, came to Salem in 1633 or 1634. Another John came to this country within a year or two of the same time, and finally settled in Connecticut, and one George came at nearly the same time and settled in Hingham. I shall try to show that these three men were at least in the old country closely connected by blood as well as by name.

First, the family look can at once be seen in the face, the forehead, the shape of the top of the head, the nose, the chin, the expression of the mouth, the carriage of the body, as well as the expression of the eyes and the arch of the eyebrow, and the firm step. In fact, as the Jew knows the Jew in all countries, speaking all languages, anywhere and everywhere, so the descendants of these three men, John the first, John the second and George, have those distinctive features that are easily known and recognized everywhere in those of mature age. I do not think all have each of these marked features, but sufficient to identify a family likeness. I recognize the fact that this similarity has existed in this country for 250 years. How many years, think you, did it exist in the old country from which we came? I conclude, therefore that without positive proof of relationship of these three men, still the circumstantial evidence to which I have

alluded and the evidence all around us to-day, speaks to each of us
of one common origin   My father is only the fifth generation from
Zachariah, the first son of the John of Salem, and all the line down
they have looked the same   I show you the likeness of some of
them, and the children of John the second and of George of Hingham will, I have no doubt, agree with me as to the correctness of the
family likeness

I see no good reason, therefore, why these two men may not have
been brothers, and one a cousin, or that all three were cousins   One
thing is true beyond a doubt, that strength and vitality of body, as
well as brain of the ancestors of these three men, were most wonder-
ful in infusing, through them all, the peculiarities that I have spoken
of, that have continued through at least five generations, and appear
distinctly to this day.   Our witty poet, Oliver Wendell Holmes,
when asked, "When should the physical training of a child com-
mence?" replied, "One hundred years before the child is born."
May not this be indeed true with our ancestors?   How has it showed
itself in our families?   Our ancestors in England must have been
very perfect men, sound in body, pure in morals, with clear untainted
blood, with an unbeclouded brain, and our ancestors in this country
have on the whole been worthy descendants of such honored sires
.If time would permit I could submit a list of many whose lives have
been extended far beyond the usual ages of men.   Let me speak of
John my ancestor and his wife and children, the state of the times
in which they lived and the peculiar phases of society

The colony at Cape Ann in 1623 and 1624, under the charge of
Mr Robert Conant, removed to a fruitful neck of land called Naumkeag, now Salem   This colony was almost a total failure.   In fact,
in order to save " by occupation" the lands granted by the patents,
known as the Dorchester company, it became necessary that another
colony should be formed, a new charter be obtained, and men of
wealth and influence interested

Mr White, the father of the first colony saw that in case a new
colony with the requisites above stated, was not at once formed, all
the work which was now being abandoned by his associates would be
lost.   He wrote to Mr Conant, faithfully promising that if he and
three others, viz., John Woodbury, John Balch, and Peter Palfreys,
would remain at Naumkeag, he would obtain a patent and forward
men and supplies ; this was agreed to   They soon after became dis-
couraged, and were ready to break this agreement.   They were finally

persuaded by Mr Conant to remain and wait the providence of God
Mr Woodbury was sent to England for supplies, thus the breath of
life was continued in the colony, and Conant and his companions
remained, the sentinels of Puritanism on the Bay of Massachusetts

Mr White was working successfully in England and obtained a
patent March 19th, 1628, conveying to Sir Henry Roswell, Sir John
Young, Thomas Southcote, John Humphrey, John Endicott, and
Simon Whitcomb, "all that part of New England lying between three
miles to the north of the Merrimac, and three miles to the south of
the Charles river, and of every part thereof, in the Massachusetts
bay," and in length between the described breadth, from the Atlantic
ocean to the South sea

Mr White being himself invincible to all opposition, several mer-
chants of London, of wealth and reputation, were induced to become
partners in the adventure   The first three of the original patentees
withdrawing, the rest purchased, or assumed their rights, formed a
company which was afterwards known as the Massachusetts company,
and organized by choosing Matthew Cradock for governor of the
company, with a board of assistants, who were the chief officers of
the company after its incorporation under the royal charter, May 30,
1628.

John Endicott, Esq , a Puritan of the sternest mould, yet possess-
ing many excellent traits, manifested much willingness to accept
their offer as soon as it was tendered, and he was appointed governor
of the plantation   The last of June, 1628, he embarked in the
Abigail, ' Henry Gauden, master " accompanied by his wife.   Not
more, and perhaps less than fifty persons accompanied him   These
and some others connected with his family, and the old planters
under Conant, in all did not exceed one hundred persons   A few
frame houses and log huts, not sufficient to accommodate less than
100 people, constituted the buildings in Salem.   Gov   Endicott
arrived in Salem, Sept 6, 1628.   The first frame house put up in
Salem, as is supposed, was placed there by Gov. Endicott, very soon
after his arrival   The house formerly stood in Cape Ann, and was
put up by the Dorchester company.

The new company in London, with ample means, commenced a
grand and comprehensive system of active work in the different parts
of the kingdom   They could not advertise in newspapers, as we do
They were dependent upon other means   The most plausible and
gifted speakers were employed to personally address the masses, ·

7

fully setting forth all the ins, and carefully avoiding the outs, incident to migration, in giving up all the comforts of home, for the uncertainty of making a new home in the deserts of Massachusetts   Many promises were made, among others that every family should have a deed of 20 acres of land, and 10 additional acres for each healthy child.   This, no doubt, was the great inducement which led so many of the poorer and well to do classes to give up the old, and seek a new home here   Governor Endicott was very wise in selecting his staff of officers, to assist him in all the departments of the government, particularly in selecting the man for the ministerial office, whose duties were to gather and organize a church and be its pastor. His choice was Rev. Samuel Skelton, of Lincolnshire   Of him it is said, he was of gracious speech, and full of faith   No doubt his eloquence and power of utterance, and his full faith in God and the work of the colony, had much to do with his and his co-laborers' success, for mainly through their efforts emigrants had been secured sufficient for a fleet of eight ships, among which were the George, the Talbot, and the Lion's Whelp   These three were to sail first, Mr Skelton and family, " wife and two daughters," in the George, Mr. Higginson with his family and Mr. Smith in the Talbot, and Mr. Bright in the Lion's Whelp.   Permission from the Lords' treasurer was obtained for the departure of 60 women and maids, 26 children and 300 men, also about 180, supposed to have been servants; with arms and tools and 140 head of cattle.   The George sailed May 4, and arrived in Salem June 23, 1629   Thus the London Plantation in the Massachusetts bay in New England, with Gov John Endicott, was the first permanent successful colony or plantation in Salem and its vicinity, which in a few years led to a union of the pilgrims and the Puritans.   The great wealth and respectability of the latter, and their character for active business, their motto being to *push things*, soon established a united colony with Gov Winthrop as its chief magistrate.   Rev Samuel Skelton and family, resided, it is said, in a log hut, or unfinished building, 20x22, with three rooms.   He commenced his work as a Christian minister   He organized a church July 30th, and August 6th the deacons chosen were ordained   Mr. Skelton was ordained pastor and Mr. Higginson was ordained teacher. There were 30 members   This is the first church of the Puritans, and the second Independent Congregational church, in America.

Will you please allow me to take up the warp and scattered thread of history and weave in my own filling, showing character, conditions and habits of the people.

Early in the summer of 1634 there were but few streets laid out in Salem. Log houses abounded, of every size and quality, one story high, with sharp thatched roofs, large stone chimneys and fire-places, usually containing three rooms beside the attic; usual size 16x20, the larger size 18x22 and 24 and some 20x26 feet. Here the well-to-do and the poor resided, the rich and the noble also occupied them until frame houses could be built. The people of the whole town were eager at work, sawing lumber and boards in the saw pits. But few frame houses were yet to be seen. One prominent for its size was owned and occupied by Gov. Endicott. Women and girls were seen everywhere cultivating ground attached to their humble houses. They were making a garden for vegetables. A few flowers could be seen here and there, showing that they had not lost their taste for the beautiful even in their poverty. They had cheerful faces and the children looked happy. There was a cluster of houses and buildings near the Clean Gravel beach, now Derby wharf. The water was clean, deep and bold, and the largest ships could anchor near the shore. There were no wharves. Salem harbor is well protected on the north by the towns of Beverly, Manchester and Gloucester, on the east by an island now called Lowell island, on the south by Marblehead. On the top of its high hill there is a beacon which signals all vessels as they approach the harbor. The signal is up, the news flies swiftly through the town. The wind is southeast, with a fresh breeze.

It is about 4 o'clock p. m., and soon a sail is seen off Marblehead's outward point. One of the company's officials quickly passes, and says the ship will be here at anchor in about an hour. The people leave their work and all, men, women and children hasten to the beach, the people gathering to welcome the coming ship, and greet the many friends who may be on board, some of them long expected, also they want the letters from near relatives and dear friends that are in England. The crowd gathers until every person of every station in life seems to be present, crowding on the beach near where the ship will cast its anchor, and land its passengers in boats, as there are no wharves. Among all classes of people, we notice first the refined, educated and well-to-do class. Although most of them are living in log houses with the scantiest amount of furniture, they are neatly dressed, and their faces are bright and hopeful, for with them it is only a matter of time when they shall unpack their furniture, now in the company's store house, and have it placed in

the comely dwellings soon to be erected for their new, beautiful homes The next class are apparently farmers in more rustic and well patched garments, they have an independent, business-like way with them, and their faces betoken confidence in themselves, and in the future The next class are the mechanics and the laboring people, who work for themselves or for wages. they seem somewhat excited, yet happy, they are coarsely clothed, their garments clean, but well worn, the women many of them have no shoes on, and some wear the wooden shoe A few wear nothing on their heads, the dark skin and straight hair, bright eyes, and comely features and healthy countenances, and quiet demeanor, indicating that some of the young Indian women have become the wives of the white man

The crowd is parting, some distinguished persons will soon be seen, the men seem to be gathering on one side and the women and children on the other The men raise their hats or their hands to their heads, and make a respectful bow The women put their right hands on their breast and make a low courtesy. Two persons now approach One is in appearance some 55 years old, with a hectic flush on his face, walking feebly His face and bearing show that he is a gentleman, his dress indicates that he is a clergyman, his waist coat covers his body, his small clothes from the waist are quite loose to the knee, and fastened there by large black buckles, his stockings are long and black, his shoes are high about the ankle, with high heels and pointed at the toe, with large black buckles on the top of the shoe, his overcoat is loose from his neck, with a flat cape like a collar and close fitting sleeves, and he has a large, high, white ruffle tied closely around his neck.

By his side is a beautiful young woman apparently about 22 years old She is a little above the medium height, with dark hair parted in the middle and carried back loosely and fastened on the top of her head with a cable-cord-like braid, revealing a broad high forehead, an intelligent face, a bright dark blue eye ; her countenance shows mingled joy and anxiety. A tear tells that she has a deep sorrow for her mother, which in the hour of her gladness cannot be entirely repressed. Her well developed form and stately bearing show that she is a lady first in rank and social position. Her dress is of Queen Elizabeth style, extreme long waist pointed in front, with belt fastened by a buckle, the skirt full over the hips and flowing nearly to the ground, pointed-toed shoes with high heels, a high ruffle around her neck fastened loosely in front, tight sleeves and ruffles on her wrist, with

only one ornament upon her person, a plain gold ring upon her left forefinger. The gentleman at her side is emaciated and feeble. Yet the likeness could not be mistaken, she must be, she is his daughter, and they gaze intently and lovingly into each other's faces and then at the ship that has already rounded the point, and is making swift progress towards the landing.

A third party now joins them with pleasant greetings. His face when once seen can never be forgotten, every feature shows that he is no ordinary man. He is of medium height, dressed as in the days of Henry the 8th—his brown velvet coat and small clothes with long stockings, high cut shoes and high heels and silver buckles, his long vest covering his body and carefully fitted to his person, his hat not unlike the Dutch hat of the times in shape, but not in stiffness, soft, and of the best material. Some very pleasant words are spoken, showing that they are on the most intimate terms. He is very complimentary and mentions the becoming dress of the young lady.

The gentleman replies that this was his departed wife's dress and has not been worn since their marriage, except on one or two occasions, that his daughter, who was nearly the same size, and so much resembled her mother, was persuaded to put it on now for the first time. He went on saying "The one we expect so soon to see and welcome, saw this costume upon my dear wife, at your reception in Lincolnshire, at the time you desired me to become a member of your council and the minister to this colony."

"Ah, I do remember it well, and how beautiful she was! and her bearing how dignified and queenly! and in all truth and frankness, I must say the mother and daughter look the same, only the mother showed a little more years, but hardly any more maturity in form or dignity of bearing. She does not hear a word I have said. No, no, her mind is intent on one she expects in a few moments to see."

Then the anchor is cast off, the flood tide is swinging the noble ship that has borne so many precious lives across the mighty ocean, and now on her stern can plainly be seen and they read her name, "Mary and John," while the bow and side of the ship are filled and crowded with passengers. The eyes of the three are steadily gazing.

"Can it be possible that he has not come? is he sick or has he died on the passage, or did he conclude to give me up?" thought the young woman, as the tears flowed over her face. "That is he, that is he!" said the happy young lady, as she wiped away her tears.

' That is your John, I mean our John," said the father.

" That is indeed your John," said the gentleman by her side, with a voice showing his deep sympathy. Then taking the hand of the father and of the daughter, he said, "I wish you much joy, my dear friends "

There stood on the quarter deck a young man who at once recognized them, taking off his hat he bowed very low three times. Many boats had now surrounded the good ship "Mary and John" and were fast taking the passengers to the shore. What a meeting as each boat landed! Friends and loved ones, parents and children, brothers and sisters, wives and husbands, each and all were seeking and embracing each other. There were some heart-rending cries of those who had come so far across the water to find that their loved ones had died, and of others who were told how their dear ones had died on the passage, and been buried in the sea; and many sad letters were received telling of sickness and death beyond the seas

In a few moments a boat was nearing the shore, the splendid form of a stalwart young man leaped on the beach, and the first footprints of a Marsh had now been made on this continent. With a firm step, but respectful demeanor, with uncovered head, revealing a broad and high forehead, well balanced with benevolence and firmness, with dark steady eyes showing that he was kind and generous but not to be trifled with, he approached the little group who had come to the water's edge to meet and bid him welcome. The clergyman, for he was Rev. Samuel Skelton, clasping the young man's hand, in his feebleness could hardly stand, but was firmly and tenderly held up by the powerful hand of the young man, while with a calm but tremulous voice and tearful eyes he bade Mr. John welcome to his new home in the wilderness and to the warm loving hearts ready to receive him. The young man turns and in a moment gives the old Norman salutation, warm kisses on each cheek, as he whispers, "My dearest Susanna." Turning to the third party of the little group he saw the extended hand, which he clasped and said, "My obedience, Governor Endicott," who quickly in his business-like way replied, "You are indeed welcome, Mr John."

At the quiet residence of the clergyman, Mr. Skelton freely talked with Mr. John and informed him that he had selected for him his quota of land 20 acres some little distance from the village, which he regarded as most desirable. The soil was most excellent, it was well covered with a valuable forest and had also water power. The title would be confirmed in their London companies office, as soon as he

had made his entry at this office, and erected some buildings and occupied the same with a wife. That he had arranged with the company for additional grants or purchases, so that he could increase his 20 acres to any number should he so desire, that he had not unpacked his furniture, which was in the company's store house Since Mrs. Skelton had died, with his own failing health and the many cares incident to his office, he had no heart to make any change

'And now Mr John we are very, very glad to see you. We have constantly thought about you and fully remembered all your manly and truthful qualities while you were my pupil at Lincolnshire, that so endeared you to all of us. Mrs. Skelton longed to see you She often said that you seemed to her already a son, and she loved to think of you as such. She left us March 15, 1631, and passed on to her heavenly home We had a most severe cold winter, there were many sick ; and out of our little number eighty had died Mrs Skelton spent her whole time in visiting the sick and afflicted, comforting the dying, as only a devoted Christian woman can do The people were not satisfied with the church prayer book They wanted warm sympathy, and prayer that came fresh from a loving heart. This Mrs. Skelton gave until worn out, her strength exhausted, she sickened and passed on to the better life, March 15, 1631. Susanna has devoted herself in trying to take her mother's place She is loved by all in this little village. Gov. Endicott greatly desired that we should have a better and more comfortable home to dwell in. Each of us said, Nay, nay, we will live as most of our people do, and keep in full sympathy with them, in their joys and sorrows The house for God's worship has not yet been commenced, we had rather remain in this loghouse where we have lived since we reached this shore and I became the minister to this people."

Only a short time and illness and feebleness increased and Mr. Skelton died August 2, 1634, and thus closed his ministry in peace.

As was the custom, the marriage of John and Susanna was deferred. In the meantime his farm was put under cultivation, a small frame house was built, which was enlarged from time to time In the autumn of 1635 they were married

A few days since I was in the building in Salem, claimed to be the first building occupied by the first church "This is a mistake, as the church occupied one or more buildings, probably log houses, from 1629 to the time they occupied this house' This church or

meeting house in size was 17x20 or 21 feet. I was *told* that it was occupied in 1634, that the first pastors were Francis Higginson, 1629 to 1630 ; Samuel Skelton, 1629 to 1634 ; Roger Williams, 1631 to 1635 The statement that all these men preached in this house is an error. Neither of them ever officiated or held public worship in this house, and for this simple reason, " *It was not built* "

Also Rev Francis Higginson died August 6, 1630, Rev Samuel Skelton died August 2, 1634, and Roger Williams was banished from Salem early in 1635 This house is said to have been built and occupied in 1634 but the facts are, the contract for building this meeting house was made November, 1634, the trees were cut in the winter of 1635 for the material, and the building was erected during that year 1635 The glazed windows were added in 1637. There are two tablets placed lately in the church for the first pastors On the first tablet the first name, as the first pastor is Rev Francis Higginson 1629 to 1630, when in fact Mr Higginson never was pastor, but only teacher. He held that office from August 6, 1629 to August 6, 1630, just 12 months to a day, and he really could have done but little teaching His time was too valuable to the company for mere teaching as a constant correspondent for the London company and writer of letters which were published and scattered broadcast over England, and they produced mighty results, as can be seen by the large number who were thus induced to emigrate He was a mighty man in speech, and also with his pen I do him all honor for his great usefulness, I would not say one word to lessen his fame, for it can hardly be overestimated I regret to see his name on the head of the tablet in that church to an office that history shows he never held Samuel Skelton was the pastor appointed July 30, and ordained August 6, 1629, and Mr. Higginson was appointed and ordained the same day as teacher, and Roger Williams was chosen teacher or assistant to Mr. Skelton after the death of Mr Higginson in 1630, and succeeded to the pastorate after the death of Mr Skelton August 2, 1634

As I reverently stood in that little 17x21 feet building " enlarged about 1639 to 17x42," memories of the past came over me In thought I saw that little church crowded It was Feb 28, 1637 At the proper stage of the services, John and Susanna Marsh brought to the baptismal font a baby boy, " he may have been several months old." The minister took the child and said as the congregation rose to their feet, and as he applied the water, " Brethren this is Zachariah Marsh the grandson of our late beloved Pastor Skelton "

The usual congratulations were tendered at the close of the service. This child was the first Marsh born in this country. This scene was repeated in the same little church in 1639, March 19th, for the 2d child John. Then here came

In 1641 March 5th, the 3d child, Ruth
In 1644, , the 4th child, Benjamin.
In 1646, Dec 3d, the 5th child, Elizabeth
In 1648, Sept. 24th, the 6th child, Ezekiel
In 1650, Aug 1st, the 7th child, Bethiah
In 1652, Sept. 2d, the 8th child, Samuel.
In 1654, March 7th, the 9th child, Susanna
In 1656, Aug 14th, the 10th child, Mary.
In 1659, Feb 16th, the 11th child, Jacob

These baptisms covered the space of 22 years, and 227 years have passed since then.

This great panorama passed before my vision, and I said where are they and all that witnessed these interesting services? They are gone. But their descendants? Some are here to-day, and thousands are scattered all over our land, and over the world, making I trust the world better for having lived.

" For we are the same our fathers have been·
We see the same sights our fathers have seen,
We drink the same stream and view the same sun,
And run the same course our fathers have run

The thought we are thinking our fathers would think,
From the death we are shrinking, our fathers would shrink;
To the life we are clinging, they also would cling,
But it speeds for us all like a bird on the wing

They loved, but the story we cannot unfold,
They scorned, but the heart of the haughty is cold,
They grieved, but no wail from their slumbers will come,
They joyed, but the tongue of their gladness is dumb

They died; ay! they died, and we things that are now,
Who walk on the turf that lies o'er their brow,
Who make, in their dwelling, a transient abode,
Meet the things that they met on their pilgrimage road.

Yea! hope and despondency, pleasure and pain,
We mingle together in sunshine and rain,
And the smiles and the tears, the song and the dirge,
Still follow each other, like surge upon surge

8

'Tis the wink of an eye, 'tis the draught of a breath,
From the blossom of health to the paleness of death,
From the gilded saloon to the bier and the shroud—
Oh, why should the spirit of mortal be proud? "

John Marsh sailed from England in 1633 and arrived in Salem
early in 1634. His son Zachariah, Married Dec. 15, 1664, Mary
Silsbee ' dau of Henry Silsbee of Salem " They had nine children,
six boys and three girls We descended from the seventh child,
Ezekiel, born in 1680 died 1750. Married Rebecca Gould July 1,
1702 They had six children, three boys and three girls. We
descended from the second child, Ezekiel born and bap May 27,
1711 Married in 1732 to Sarah Buffington who was born 1716 and died
1809. He died 1798, 88 years old They had five children three
boys and 2 girls Then fourth child John was born May 26, 1750.
This commences a separate line of our family as to-day here repre-
sented. He married Frances Foster of Marblehead, and died July
30, 1778. She died July 27, 1808 They had two sons, both
named John, the oldest died in infancy. The second John born Nov.
26, 1778, married Aug 22, 1798, Mary Brown, born Dec. 23, 1772.
They had seven children, five boys and two girls. The third child
James born March 7, 1803, married, April 5, 1825, Mary P. Felton,
and they have had seven children, one girl and six boys Hon James
Marsh now in his 84th year, with his wife and gifted daughter Hannah Felton Marsh and two of his stalwart sons, we have the great
pleasure of welcoming to-day Caleb is the fifth child born May 3,
1834. He Married Dec 31, 1854 Clara E Brown, and they have
three children and four grandchildren Francis the other son with us,
is their seventh child, born Aug. 18, 1838, married Feb. 13, 1867 to
Catherine E. Pope They own and occupy the house and farm that
was my grandfather's residence, where my father was born July 9,
1776, and where I was born April 18, 1818 To go back to the point
of union, Ezekiel Marsh to whom I have referred, born May 27, 1711
then ancestor was my great grandfather. He was commissioned by
Gov. Wm Shirley Ensign 5th Regt. Capt. John Proctor, Col. Ichabod Plaisted, Aug 21, 1754, 28th year of the reign of his Majesty
King George 2d. Ezekiel Marsh the son of the above named, born
in Danvers Jan. 26, 1740, was my grandfather. He moved to Maine
in 1818 and died in Fairfield, Me., Sept. 15, 1822, 83 years old.
He was commissioned Lieutenant June 3, 1773 by Governor Thomas
Hutchinson in the 13th year of his Majesty King George 3d, omit-

ting to take the usual oath of allegiance. He married Abiah " or Bethiah " Hartshorn of Salem, sister of Captain Thomas Hartshorn who greatly distinguished himself during the war of 1775 to 1783. They had seven children, three boys and four girls. The sixth child Thomas H. Marsh, born July 9, 1776, was my father. He died in Fairfield, Oct 20, 1870, aged 94 years, 3 months and 11 days I have Mr. President too full a history of our family to give all now, but at a proper time I will furnish you with more Thanking you all for your patience and kind attention, let me say that the commissions to which I have referred, can be seen, as I have them here with me Again thanking you all I will close by saying that I am most happy to be present with you to-day.

HYMN SUNG AT TWO REUNIONS

TUNE—*America*

1633—1885

From England's sea girt land
By God's high guiding hand,
Our fathers sailed
They laughed at ocean's roar,
They found a broader shore,
And here forevermore
They freedom hailed

John Marsh was one of them,
Those ancient, stalwart men,
Their God their king
His Bible was his chart,
With wisest master art,
He put it in his heart
More light to bring

And George of Hingham came,
And many a queenly dame,
And lovely bride
And Marshes, as the leaves,
Or golden harvest sheaves,
Or drops that drip from eaves,
They multiplied

The women toiled and spun,
A daily task was done
By girl and son
The Marshes grew and spread,
The Marshes loved and wed,
The Marshes fought and bled,
And freedom won

Now Marsh, be merriest man,
That ever walked or ran,
Or kissed a bride,
For Marshes come and go,
As come the rain and snow,
The Marshes ebb and flow,
A little span

We boast no nobler name,
No bluer blood we claim,
Lest pride should fall,
Yet love we this our tree,
And come from land and sea
One gathering here to be,
And honor all

Two hundred years have taught,
That every Marshman ought
To live for right,
To spend his little span
In doing what he can
To serve his God and Man
With all his might

Amherst, July 22, 1885   D. W. M

Printed in the USA
CPSIA information can be obtained
at www.ICGtesting.com
LVHW010730260923
759253LV00004B/40